THE BL

THE BLUE NOTEBOOK:
Reports on Canadian Culture

DOUG FETHERLING

MOSAIC PRESS
OAKVILLE   NEW YORK   LONDON

Canadian Cataloguing in Publication Data

Fetherling, Doug, 1949 –
  The blue notebook: reports on Canadian culture

Includes index.
ISBN 0-88962-320-1

1. Authors, Canadian — 20th century - Addresses, essays, lectures. 2.
Canada — Intellectual life — 20th century — Addresses, essays, lectures.
I. Title.

PS8077.F47 1985   C810'.9'0054   C85-099575-2
PR9189.6.F47 1985

Published by Mosaic Press, P.O. Box 1032, Oakville, Ontario, L6J 5E9,
Canada. Offices and Warehouses, 1252 Speers Rd., Unit 10, Oakville,
Ontario, L6L 5N9, Canada.

Published with the assistance of the Canada Council and the Ontario Arts
Council.

Cover design by Rita Vogel.
Typeset by Lount Press Graphics.
Printed and bound in Canada.

ISBN 0-88962-320-1 paper

Mosaic Press:
  In the U.S.,   Flatiron Book Distributors, 1170 Broadway, Suite 807, New
                 York, N.Y., 10001, U.S.A.

  In the U.K.,   John Calder (Publishers) Ltd., 18 Brewer Street, London,
                 W1R 4AS, England

  In Australia, Bookwise International, 1 Jeanes Street, Beverley, South
                 Australia, 5007, Australia

By the same author

Variorum: New Poems and Old, 1965–1985
The Five Lives of Ben Hecht
Gold Diggers of 1929
A George Woodcock Reader (editor)

For Howard Engel and Janet Hamilton

PREFACE

For many years now I have been inordinately fond of a type of book that seems to grow less common with the passage of time, though it is one still comparatively popular in Britain: the book of collected or selected "pieces." Such assemblages of old reviews and review articles, often masquerading as essays, usually carry a preface in which the author denigrates the tradition. His thrust is that the stuff to follow is so much cold broth, mere journalism, dated now but resurrected here for reasons both indistinct and suspect. Custom demands lip service to the logic shown by GBS when he informed a correspondent, "I cannot bring myself to republish my articles. They appear very entertaining in the context of the week in which they appear, but just because they are good journalism, they are bad literature." In this case what follows may not even be good journalism. Its claim is only that it sets out one observer's impressions of recent Canadian culture, defining culture broadly enough to include such matters as feature films and political cartoons.

Since the 1960s I have laboured mostly as a cultural and political journalist, the sort known in the nineteenth century as a magazinist. The job has included spending perhaps two years with one periodical as a regular book reviewer, three years with another as film columnist, and so on, usually as a free lance but occasionally in some staff position, helping to get the publication out each month. It's not much of a living though it's not a bad life. One's admiration for the masters of the profession, Sir J.C. Squire for instance, can only increase when one sees at close range all the difficulties, such as the whims of fashion, the transience (and intransigence) of editors, the lack of space (always the lack of space) and the limitations of the medium itself. At length a particularly congenial outlet, such as I found for a few years at *Saturday Night*, may open up. Even then there is little scope for seriousness beyond what the writer can work in by subterfuge or plain good fortune. But in adopting the form one adapts it as best one can. In terms of books and literature, for example, such journalism is not well suited to discussing language, but it is quite handy for commenting on the texture of people's careers, and is thus a useful means of looking at the temper of the times and the passing spectacle.

For the most part the period covered here is the 1970s. The personalities include older figures in their prime and others then new to prominence. Those years now seem to have been a watershed in Canada's cultural life.

In literature, for instance, a new generation of fiction writers came together and regional voices found national audiences at last. In publishing as well as in film and other fields, much of the cultural infrastructure was quickly built up and then just as quickly reassessed. But I say this only to provide background and without any suggestion that the following reports and reviews form a survey of even the highest-relief spots. Usually I have had no single perch from which to write consistently about the broad sweep of events or about all the major players; even if I had, I would still have preferred commenting on what most stimulated my own curiosity and that of my editors.

As I have gone about my duties I have sometimes been struck by the opportunities for dealing with a given topic from different angles, and have often wondered whether individual notices, considered in sequence, might reveal unexpected patterns or otherwise justify themselves. Eventually it became my practice to take clippings of certain pieces and stuff them between the leaves of an old spiral-bound notebook with blue covers, in the hope that one day they might be useful. Looking at the notebook again recently, I saw that its contents, if put in some logical order, purged of needless repetitions and with a few old deletions restored, might make a small contribution to this favourite form of mine and show how the subjects discussed here appeared at the time. The ambition is as modest as the vessel that contains it.

ONE:
F.P. Grove Versus F.P. Greve

i

Douglas O. Spettigue relates in *FPG: The European Years* the story of
Frederick Philip Grove's winning a Governor General's Award in 1947 for his
semi-fictional autobiography *In Search of Myself*. Grove was crippled by a
stroke and unable to travel to Ottawa to receive the honour, so it was delivered
to him by William Arthur Deacon, the tweedy book editor of *The Globe and
Mail*. When Grove received it, he wept. The story has been around for some
time (Deacon told it on a CBC Grove symposium in 1962, when academic
interest in the man was just beginning). But until the appearance of
Spettigue's work, one of the most revealing Canadian literary studies of recent
years, it was unclear exactly why he had wept.

Spettigue doesn't say. But, by filling in many of the gaps and straightening
many of the crooked truths in the novelist's past, he certainly allows for a
reasonable guess. Grove cried, those few short months before his death,
not out of happiness and excitement at his years of ceaseless effort finally
being recognized by the deans of his adopted country. He cried in irony
because Canada — to him, probably, this pitifully Philistine place without
history — had recognized him long after the true promise of his first career
had been forgotten; forgotten in Europe where it had happened, not in Canada
where, until recently, no one had even guessed at its existence.

Spettigue's interest in Grove began when he was a graduate student in
the 1950s, and *FPG: The European Years* is the result of six years' research.
Its basic revelations are that Grove was in fact Felix Paul Greve, who published
several novels and a whole shelf of translations before coming to North
America (in 1909, not 1892 as he himself wrote) after serving time in Bonn
for fraud, deserting his first wife and allowing suicide to be inferred from his
disappearance. That much Spettigue first showed in a 1972 article in *The
Queen's Quarterly*, following up an earlier contribution in which he set straight
errors in his 1969 monograph on Grove. The present book gives still more
new information and theorizes at some length on its implications as well as
on the gaps that remain. Its effect is to make Grove, hitherto and still one
of your less intrinsically interesting Canadian writers, at the very least a quite
interesting man. By pulling the rug from beneath those who have hinted at
the implausibility of Grove's own story as well as those who never questioned
it, Spettigue has effected a *coup* in the small world of Canadian literary
scholarship and come out on top in the still-smaller one of Grove studies.

Grove's version ran (with frequent variations) that he had been born in 1879 in what he sometimes called a mansion in Russia, through which his Swedish parents (sometimes his mother was Scots) had been passing. Spettigue shoots this down by proving he was born in what was then Poland, to undeniably German parents. He also refutes many of the other facts Grove was to dole out about his family and his life in the old country. For instance, Grove never studied in Paris and at Oxford, as he later claimed, but lived rather in worlds even more fascinating than the ones he concocted. Indeed, as intriguing as are the lies in which Spettigue catches his subject, they are not nearly so intriguing as the brand-new truths.

When Grove was growing up, the eighteenth century still lived on in education. A knowledge of classical languages and travel about the Continent were still crucial, and Greve, a not badly off kid, enjoyed them. He even studied Sanskrit which, though of understandably little use in later life, says something for the linguistic abilities that served him in making a living. It is here that the incongruity sets in. Young Greve could have entered into "eventually perhaps the respectability of a professorship somewhere" but was drawn instead by force of his temperament into the atmosphere of bohemian decadence. He became a notable rogue, rake and bounder, patterning himself after Oscar Wilde, on whom he wrote or translated ten works in the space of a year and a half. A damned lively individual, Greve, and the major obstacle one faces in mentally linking the two personalities comes not from doubting any of Spettigue's detective work, but from reconciling this Teutonic literary charlatan with the bucolic codger of twenty years later who penned *Over Prairie Trails*.

Spettigue shows that Grove romanticized what was anyway a very romantic background. In the autobiography, for instance, Grove wrote that he hob-nobbed in Paris with the likes of Mallarmé, but Spettigue proves that at the time Grove would have had to have been a schoolboy of eleven; it is known, however, that Greve enjoyed several curious meetings with André Gide, for Gide left records of them. This was at the time Greve was on the make, in a hurry to be famous, and Spettigue speculates that Greve may have hinted at offering sexual favours in exchange for professional boosts — a trick for which the wily old Gide did not fall.

After serving a year in prison for attempting to defraud a friend of a fair amount of money and after taking it on the lam transatlantically, Grove (who used at least five pseudonyms) had good reason to cover his tracks. And for a literary man, one used to turning experience to account, he did a rather good job. Beyond this, as an artist he probably saw little harm in turning personal history into more valuable if less accurate art; "his most evident characteristic" was "a capacity for bluff"; he "made every effort to have fact and fiction coincide wherever possible"; he was, in short, a subscriber to the school of writing whose contention it is that you should never let the facts interfere with a good story.

Greve's first wife — with whom he lived in sin before marrying, an outrage at the time — remains a nearly complete mystery, and in general Spettigue has learned more about his subject's career than about his personal life, and has done so partly through the efforts of German scholars: at the time Spettigue and others were puzzling over Grove's past, they were asking themselves whatever became of Greve. Although Greve published a few novels beginning in 1903 and likely would have fulfilled his larger ambitions, he supported his foppery by toiling as a translator. He prepared renderings of not only Wilde and Gide but Browning, Wells, Flaubert, Murger, Swift, "Junius" and Dickens. At one point Spettigue uses the figure of more than 12,000 pages of published translations, some of which are still in print today. Greve even translated some of *The Arabian Nights*, employing not one of the numerous expurgated versions but that nobly complete one by Sir Richard Burton. Translation was, however, an ill-paid profession, and when events took their course he left a "suicide" message and booked passage for the United States and Canada. He was then thirty years old, not nineteen, twenty or twenty-four, as he would say later.

Spettigue is a reliable scholar but he suffers from a fault Grove noticed in a fellow translator — "he still addresses the understanding, not the ear . . ." It is possible to do both, and Spettigue might have taken a lesson from *The Quest For Corvo* without jeopardizing his scholarship. He tells almost nothing of his search, except to say that Grove's identity came to him one day in the British Museum.

There is some uncertainty about the audience for which *FPG: The European Years* is intended. While certain concessions are made in the presentation of material (at least in the first part of the book), Spettigue presupposes, above and beyond a sincere interest on the part of his readers, a pretty thorough knowledge of Grove's Canadian works, not all of which are in print. It may be guessed that as his monograph and articles were a stepping-stone to this work, so this work might be a bridge to a full biography, though not before a great deal more research. Grove or Greve still has three missing years in his life (1909 to 1912) and, in theory anyway, this makes him in academic terms three-sevenths as good a subject as Shakespeare.

The immediate impact of *FPG: The European Years* is considerable. Spettigue is now off following a lead on the transitory Polish stage of Greve's life and is busy with A.W. Riley, head of the German department at Queen's University, where Spettigue teaches, translating Greve's early novels into English. Already Spettigue has written an introduction to a new reprint of *In Search of Myself*. He has become the Leon Edel of Frederick Philip Grove studies, outstripping Ronald Sutherland and Margaret Stobie, authors of two other Grove monographs, and Desmond Pacey, the editor of Grove's letters and fugitive stories, to say nothing of various writers of theses, papers and pieces. The true importance of all this, however, is that we know now that Grove culled some of his Canadian fiction from his European, not his Prairie experience; that he was a much more accomplished and established literary figure and fabricator than we had imagined; that his personality, which formerly vied with some of his works for a claim on one's inattention, is more interesting by reason of being more complex; and that he was, again, not a Swede but a German, who went to great pains to hide the fact long before it became fashionable to do so.

Saturday Night, 1974

ii

Present-day Canadian writers who read the correspondence of Frederick Philip Grove may well be overtaken by a wave of *déjà vu*. They may also sense that they're reading about themselves or at least about some of their contemporaries. *The Letters of Frederick Philip Grove,* edited by Desmond Pacey shortly before his death last July, suggests that the 1920s literary life was remarkably similar to the one we have now, and that it produced many of the same quirks of personality. The Grove revealed in these personal and business communications was a man of wide acquaintanceship but few friends, who thought he was a shrewd businessman but wasn't, who was self-pitying when in neglect and more than a little arrogant when in the limelight. Like some of his successors, he didn't get on well with his publishers, who he believed were cheating him, or with his fellow novelists, whom he looked upon as unworthy competitors. A bit of Frederick Philip Grove, alas, lives on in all of us. That is one reason why this collection is a fine entertainment as well as a valuable work of scholarship.

Running beneath this continuity, however, is another more topical concern. Thanks largely to the detective work of Douglas O. Spettigue, it is now known with some certainty that Grove was not, as he claimed, a Swedish immigrant who arrived in the United States in 1892 and later came to Canada. It's known that he was actually Felix Paul Greve, a German bohemian and Grub Streeter who abandoned his wife early in the present century after serving a prison term for fraud. Evidence points to the conclusion that he came here much later, about 1912, but possibly as early as 1909, to take up a new identity, a new life and even a new spouse — his second or possibly his third, since he may have committed bigamy in the States before landing in Toronto. As useful as it is in bringing life to the character known as Grove, this collection is more interesting still, if perhaps more subtle, in shedding light on the personality of his predecessor Greve, who was also in some ways his nemesis.

These Grove letters, as Pacey pointed out, "are seldom the products of a man with his guard down." Several times, however, Grove comes perilously close to divulging the truth about himself: that he was a literary man of some reputation when disgrace forced him to fake suicide and leave the Continent. He does this mainly in his correspondence with publishers, when he hints that he was used to better things in Europe than they were offering him here. As for his personal correspondence, it is here that he seems to betray, if not the facts of his hidden life, then at least the spirit of it.

He was, Pacey has written, "by far the most erudite Canadian novelist yet to appear," and his letters reveal a broad acquaintance with mathematics, natural history, the hard sciences, the classics and European literature — or at least with European literature up to the time of his hurried emigration. With more recent writing he was less at home. He saw nothing in Gertrude Stein or Virginia Woolf and implied only the most grudging respect for D.H. Lawrence and James Joyce. Eliot he found interesting if somewhat wrong-headed. These references come in letters to his few intellectual friends in Canada. In letters intended for his wife's eyes only he was less aesthetic and secretive and more emotional and nostalgic. A glimpse he had of the aristocratic existence in Ottawa made life in that city seem "full of reminiscences" and put him, for a few hours, "quite back in my heyday of Europe."

These letters to Catherine Grove form the bulk of the edition. They arise from his cross-Canada lecture tours in 1927 and 1928, when he wrote her at least daily and, on one memorable date, sent her three letters and a wire to boot. The style of these letters shows a sentimental and loving man who was also condescending. Their content reflects Grove at the peak of his success in the new land. The success, however, was short-lived. It is doubly ironic in view of the renown he had enjoyed earlier in Europe and of the pitiful poverty and degradation that would mark his last years in Canada.

Grove was fleeing both from the self-inflicted shame of his conviction and sentence and from the threat of further prosecution. It is also reasonable to assume that at least one layer of his disguise was applied because of the anti-German sentiment then widespread in Canada and particularly evident in Manitoba, where he taught school for many years. Grove's resolve to create a new life caused him to take his teaching jobs much more seriously than one would expect and much more seriously than do most other writers who are also teachers. Soon, though, like the jade carver in the Lin Yutang story, Grove allowed his artistic impulses to get the better of him. He began writing again, or at least making his writing public. The success of his early books and the subsequent speaking dates brought out many of the resentments he felt about the time and position he had lost through indiscretion. These resentments manifested themselves in a ruthless quest for status. He was proud of having dined with old Laurier; he was even proud of having just missed dining with Mackenzie King. He took delight in berating hotel keepers for providing less than European-style service and appointments, and he even began charging for his autograph.

What Grove wanted was to be a national institution, feeling perhaps that such eminence would restore his self-respect and relieve his homesickness.

But such was not the scenario. The literary community he helped foster (he worked briefly for Graphic Publishers of Ottawa) underwent very difficult days early in the Depression. His lumbering novels, which appeared to be exercises in a kind of rural Dreiserian naturalism, passed from fashion. Grove became bitter. "There is no greater curse that can befall a man," he wrote a friend in 1941, "than to be afflicted with artistic leanings, in Canada." He added at about this same time that "it is a miracle I have survived so far, with the help of one or two diminutive wind-falls." The next year found him advertising in *Saturday Night* his willingness, for a fee, to "read, criticize, edit manuscripts, and advise re publication." There were few if any takers. In 1944 he received a sorely needed $100 from the Canadian Authors' Foundation, a charitable body now named the Canadian Writers' Foundation.

The figure of Grove in decline is more appealing than the figure of him in ascent because of the quiet dedication and integrity he exhibited under fire. He retained his pomposity, of course. He slavered after election to the Royal Society of Canada but when, on the third try, he finally received this honour, he found he lacked the necessary fifty dollars in fees. But though he complained about his penury he did not necessarily exaggerate it. He read with humbling effect the autobiography of Emily Carr, who was his superior both as an artist and a pauper. A good measure of Grove's bravery is found in a letter he sent as an old man to Lorne Pierce of the Ryerson Press. He wrote Dr Pierce (as he always addressed him, with characteristic formality) to state that a particular manuscript would be delayed. Grove's typewriter ribbon was worn out and he couldn't afford a replacement. Therefore he was typing over each line three times in order to make a readable copy.

Grove, as he revealed in these letters, was a person given to arrogance and paranoia — arrogance in thinking he knew more about publishing than his publishers did, paranoia in his fear and dislike of such contemporaries as Wilson MacDonald, Morley Callaghan and Mazo de la Roche. But in addition to these qualities he exhibited a fine moral courage and a dignity which come to light only now. Indeed, the great surprise in this edition by Pacey, who wrote on Grove intermittently for thirty years and who seemed to resent a bit Spettigue's more dramatic scholarship, is that it animates its subject in a way one would not have thought possible. *The Letters of Frederick Philip Grove* reveals more of the man than any other volume by or about him. Grove (with good reason, he must have believed) never wrote livelier, more revealing, more direct or more honest prose than he did in these sometimes careless letters to his carefully selected friends and antagonists.

Saturday Night, 1976

iii

Felix Paul Greve's second novel, *The Master Mason's House*, was first published in Germany in 1906, when its author was an ill-paid, twenty-seven-year-old translator and man of letters. Its appearance now in English is an event that positively oozes irony. Greve, who got in a jam and fled to Canada to become Frederick Philip Grove, must be in his grave not laughing but shaking his head. When he arrived in this country a few years after the book was published, it was with the intention — indeed, the necessity — of beginning afresh his literary career. He worked hard if not always well. The poverty he endured was real, the neglect he felt sometimes merely imagined. At his death his place in Canadian writing was secure, and since then it has only grown. His life was troubled but, at his passing, his reputation at least was in order. Now, with this edition, that reputation has been thrown into chaos.

The anarchic process began a few years ago when Douglas Spettigue, in his articles and his book *FPG: The European Years*, showed that Grove (known only in Canada) and Greve (only in Germany) were the same person. It was a conclusion with broad implications. For one thing, it showed the dull fellow called Grove to have been in fact an interesting man — felon, poseur, literary huckster. He seemed all the more fascinating for the conscientiousness with which, as a Canadian, he had hidden his past. For another, it meant that his literary ideas were firmly rooted in a tradition to which he had earlier seemed only indirectly obliged. Suddenly, where there had been none before, a strong link existed between Canadian literature and the artistic turmoil of Europe during the early years of the century.

Richard Ihle is the master mason in the title of Greve's book. He lives in a small, neat city in Pomerania, on the south shore of the Baltic Sea, in what was then a part of Prussia. He is an authoritarian man trying to keep up the appearance of belonging to a higher class. He has two servants and a decorous parlour and gives the impression of being another of the prosperous, middle-class artisans so popular in European fiction of the period. He lives there with his wife, Bertha, age thirty-five, and their two daughters, Susie and Lottie. When the novel begins, in 1888, Susie, the principal character, is thirteen.

It is clear that Grove was superimposing part of his own childhood upon the Susie character, with imaginative additions to make her a convincing female creation. That is part of the novel's interest, for though Spettigue linked Grove with Greve he did not succeed in learning much about Greve's personality and upbringing. Whatever else it does, the novel fills in some of the blanks, at least in pencil. It must be from memory, for instance, that Grove describes small personal events as well as larger public ones. He writes of the agony and tedium of piano lessons as though he, too, spent hours stumbling through little staccato exercises. He writes of the death of the beloved Emperor William I, and its effect upon the fictional household, in a way doubtless true to his own recollection.

Susie, a precocious schoolgirl, grows up just as her mother deteriorates.

Bertha Ihle, trapped between her husband's coldness and the sterility of her role as *Hausfrau*, lapses into depression. In 1892, she tries committing suicide by jumping off a bridge, but the river is frozen over, and she merely slides across the ice in an undignified fashion. Here is a double realization of just how poor her mental health had become — the fact that she would try killing herself and the fact that she would go about it so stupidly. After the suicide attempt she is confined to an asylum.

Her husband now sees the error of his ways. It is a further tragedy that he can make amends only in a selfish and harmful manner. He marries the widow of a consular official, a high-toned lady who is all the things he had forced his first wife to pretend she was. The new member of the family, her cavalier attitudes based on class rather than pretence, immediately begins lording it over Susie, now seventeen and too old for such bossing. The experience makes Susie reassess her father in a kinder light at times. He once or twice assumes the position of her real mother incarnate, while in her mind the stepmother becomes the symbol of unpredictable and callow authority. At base, however, Richard Ihle remains what he was before. Remembering what he did to her mother, Susie grows away from him emotionally.

In an obvious way, *The Master Mason's House* (the original title was *Maurermeister Ihles Haus*) is an early feminist novel from what seems that long ago time when women allowed as how feminist was a neuter noun. By present-day standards it seems to fail, in that its style is one we expect to see used on a broader canvas. Its value as literature, however, is less than its value as literary history.

The novel contains several elements Greve would continue struggling with as Grove — the conflict of generations, the disastrous effects of money and pretence, the slow disintegration of a once strong personality into diffuse instability. Those themes lend credence to the view (suggested by Spettigue's earlier research) that much of Grove's writing was based on European rather than Prairie observations. None of those facts, however, is so important as the book's style.

Greve was writing at a time when many important schools of literature were lumped together in an amorphous concept of Art, which stood in opposition to everything that was genteel, staid and official in culture. Greve's first prose volume, in 1903, was a study of Oscar Wilde, many of whose works he translated into German. Greve was impressed with the literary decadents, just as he is known to have been interested in the symbolist poets. Like so many writers of the time, he found those interests a natural companion to impressionism, whereby a personalized outline suggests the whole, and expressionism, the style in which mood and atmosphere are themselves important characters. Such expressionism, pretty much a German idea, was the dressed-up offspring of naturalism, by which writers attempted to take literature back into the streets, where it had flourished in the time of the oral tradition, before literacy, the privilege of the educated minority, intervened. Naturalistic writers strove for power and intimacy through vividness. The vividness was to be obtained by what seems today an over-reliance on tiny, realistic detail. It is from that tradition that Greve was writing. It is one in which he continued to work, in watered-down form, when he became a Canadian. By that time, his ideas of literature were far removed from their origins both in geography and time.

In his Canadian work Grove always seemed neither originator nor exemplar. He seemed, in a word, clumsy. If *The Master Mason's House* in a few places reads even more like a translation from the German that it is, it also reads less like the Grove we know than someone else. The author was closer to his tradition, as well as to the source of his inspiration, than was the author of *The Master of the Mill* and *Over Prairie Trails*.

In their introduction, Spettigue and A.W. Riley indicate that the translation has excised some "occasional impressionistic set-pieces . . . distinguished by a shift to the historical-present tense and by abandoning the verbs altogether" and has altered much of the odd punctuation: devices that were less Greve's own than that of the jumbled decadent-impressionist-expressionist-naturalistic tradition from which he came. Such touches as the translation has left only emphasize that, by immigration at least, Canada can now claim a part in the experimental goings-on that were so important in Britain, the United States and elsewhere. But the truly marvellous aspect of *The Master Mason's House* — which at times is a sensitive web of prose, at others a sort of Teutonic Hugh Garner — is that it shows where Grove fits in, not only in transatlantic cross-pollination but, symbolically, in the writing of his adopted country. Once he seemed only a misshapen lummox exemplifying all that was awkward and strained in the realistic, European-based, Hemingwayesque tradition that Morley Callaghan, for example, often shows at its best. Now, however, it is clear that he was one of the many legitimate practitioners, not merely a disciple who lacked the moxie. *The Master Mason's House* does not show that Greve was a better stylist than Grove, but it shows that they both wrote the way they did in light of the background they shared.

Saturday Night, 1976

TWO:
GEORGE WOODCOCK
PAST AND PRESENT

i

In Sir Herbert Read's native Yorkshire, marking the grave wherein he was placed just short of what would have been his seventy-sixth birthday, there is a stone with his name and below that the words: KNIGHT, POET, ANARCHIST. He was also biographer, memoirist, essayist, sometime painter and occasional playwright and general man of letters. *The Green Child*, though his sole published novel, remains an important one, and he was influential and untiring as an educational reformer and as a critic of society, literature and, most notably, art. Such occupations were not mutually exclusive. Even his anarchist principles and his acceptance, in 1953, of a knighthood were possibly connected in a way few readers realize. As a man of so many skills and interests, Read was forced to admit in 1968, the year of his death, that "in dissipating my talents in half-a-dozen fields I have made it difficult for my contemporaries to recognise the underlying unity of my purpose and my practice." He hoped that someday someone would take the trouble to bring it all together. George Woodcock has done just that in *Herbert Read: The Stream and the Source*, the concluding volume of what is actually a critical trilogy on Woodcock's early mentors, men whose overall achievements suggest the pattern of his own career.

Herbert Read: The Stream and the Source is not a biography. Woodcock calls it a pre-biography, a sorting out and linking together of various aspects of Read's work preparatory to a biographical narrative by someone else. Its approach, then, is not much different from those of Woodcock's books on Orwell (*The Crystal Spirit*, 1966) and Huxley (*Dawn and the Darkest Hour*, 1972) except for its ground-breaking spirit arising from the fact that Read, when Woodcock began, had not already been surveyed to death like the other two. Although the quality of the discussion is uniformly high, the quality of the writing is uneven. This is in common with the Huxley study but it contrasts with *The Crystal Spirit*, which was something of an *essai-poulet*: Woodcock admired Orwell's only sometimes successful striving for "prose like a window-pane" and in speaking about him approximated the master in what quite possibly is Woodcock's best sustained piece of writing.

The Crystal Spirit began with a section in which Woodcock reminisced about the man as he knew him, and got that quickly out of the way while also setting the mood. In the Read book he devotes the opening chapter to a sketch of the subject's life but lets his own recollections dribble out, mainly when he discusses Read's association with London anarchists during the war. In neither book, nor in the one on Huxley, does he come out and say flatly what it was about these men that was important to him and that caused him to undertake these labours on behalf of not only writing but their personal shades. The answer is there, in all three books, but in the Read especially.

Woodcock, who is one of Canada's most important natural resources, was born in Winnipeg but passed his childhood near the Welsh border in an area seemingly removed in time from the rest of 1920s Britain. It was, in its rural proximity to history, like Read's own childhood of a generation before; and if this was not an actual link in their twenty-five-year friendship, it was something the two writers had in common temperamentally. For Read, so much the cultural cosmopolitan, remained in part the contemplative country lad. Towards the end he often bemoaned the fact that his international teaching and lecturing chores left him little time for poetry — the poetry which, with his anti-Utopian novel and his autobiography *The Contrary Experience*, Woodcock calls the works by which Read will likely be remembered.

Woodcock's first meeting with Read was in the early 1940s. Woodcock was editing the little magazine *Now* and was immersing himself in the politics of anarchism, the philosophy Read had followed since the First World War, his service in which inspired some of his most interesting verse and perhaps the best section of *The Contrary Experience*. Woodcock also was establishing himself as a poet and critic and part of the far-reaching literary circle of the type London had not seen since Bloomsbury and has not witnessed since. Shortly after meeting Read he began another long friendship, with Orwell. It was only a quarter century after returning at the end of the decade to Canada, where most of his forty or so books have been written, that Woodcock turned to the large task of evaluating the, to him, triumvirate of Orwell, Read and Aldous Huxley, the third a man I do not believe he actually knew, at least not in England, but who was also influential in shaping his mind and writing.

Woodcock is this country's foremost man of letters, but not in the sense of the genteel amateur who keeps his hand in and is careful lest he dirty it with unsafe opinions of contemporaries or with tainted money derived from professional authorship. Rather he is a working polymath, who through discipline, adrenalin and amazing skill keeps track of his time's standards — standards maintained by himself as well as expected of others. This takes, for a start, a driving interest in the intellectual elements common to the arts, politics and sometimes even the sciences; it is not a question of being an adjudicator or propagandist but of being a sifter, a dissecter and explainer and ultimately a disseminator of ideas. In Orwell this was an obvious attraction, and in Huxley Woodcock saw a man working in "a continental tradition, that of the *homme de lettres.* . . ." So, too, it is not surprising to discover Woodcock telling us: "Read, in other words, was a true Man of

Letters, in the sense understood in France and other European countries, of a writer who refuses to accept a hierarchy of forms, but is willing to turn his talents to any use that does not compromise his integrity." There are of course dangers in this, which Woodcock knows and has himself tried to avoid. Read's problem was not that he spread himself too thin but that he spread himself rather unwisely.

Read's career as a poet began when he was in university, before the First World War. His early training was under the imagists, a fact that helps explain something Woodcock does not touch on — Read's long championing, decades later, of that most European of the Beats, Denise Levertov, who is a far cry from anyone else whose poetry he ever liked enough to praise. Certainly by the end of his final *Collected Poems* there is little if any trace of the influence of Pound or Aldington or Aldington's wife, H.D. Early in life Read was also a painter. Stronger evidence aside, the fact that in sixty years of writing he commented relatively little on contemporary poetry and a great deal on contemporary art meant that he was much more poet than artist and remained so to the end. This fact, as well as the type of art criticism Read did, helps tell us — specifically, beyond Woodcock's general definition — what kind of man of letters he was.

Unlike Orwell, Read was not a great reporter, who felt compelled to comment on the stream of culture flowing past him, and unlike Woodcock he was not a cultural historian and investigator, whose task it is to take apart culture and compare it with other culture. He was rather, as Woodcock suggests, "one of the great generalizing intelligences of our age." Although at times this handicapped his literary criticism, it gave him a vision that set apart his writing on the fine arts from other people's. Plus, of course, the fact that he actually had an eye for painting and sculpture, was able to view them as a fellow artist would and was able to report on them from that rather than from the outsider's or true reporter's standpoint.

Read's generalizing intelligence made him a placer of things in broad contexts: he was what might be called an aerial rather than terrestrial or even amphibious critic. Strangely, I think, for such a person, he was an incessant rewriter and rearranger of his own work. Woodcock's bibliography lists well over 100 books and pamphlets by Read, many of them revised or expanded versions, but relatively few of Read's editions of and prefaces to other people's work, about which Kenneth Clark reportedly once joked. (If the Nazis actually had invaded Britain, reasoned Lord Clark, himself no mean prefacer, and had sorted out seditious books for burning in the streets, the stack of works published in the past ten years with forewords by Read would have been higher than the stack published in the past decade *without* Read introductions.) The book list also shows beyond a doubt that most of Read's writing energy went into art, particularly during the second half of his career, and particularly the modern art of his generation which he did so much to make respectable and which he lived to see regarded as neoclassic.

Specifically he wrote a number of books both critical and general on groups of artist friends such as Henry Moore and Ben Nicholson.

Woodcock makes the point that Read's more general art books, his surveys and particularly his *Education Through Art* — which caused a small revolution in teaching and was the seed of the UN-affiliated Society for Education Through Art — were Read's true contribution to anarchist decentralization. Such books as *Anarchy and Order* notwithstanding, he wrote no strictly libertarian texts of great importance, nor did he approach Woodcock's considerable role as an analyst of the movement and its main historian. His whole career as an anarchist, in fact, remains highly ambivalent, at times even naïve, despite Woodcock's hard work at making it seem less so.

A pacifist through participation in the First World War, he supported Britain's involvement in the Second World War; and on a 1959 visit to China he found in the communes something close to anarchism in action, not mentioning that the Red Army, though it does not distinguish between officers and men, is an army just the same. And his acceptance of the knighthood of Elizabeth II brought an international howl from his fellows; Woodcock and Augustus John were alone in defending him on the grounds that anarchist freedom to choose means also freedom to choose even in matters such as that (though it is significant that Woodcock has refused the Order of Canada). The truth, I think, is that Read found in anarchism too much of what kept him from commenting on current poetry. He was interested in the principles but for him the attempts at practice entailed too much politics and the knowledge that no one person agreed completely with any other. Read felt more at home in areas where his aerial view and historical inclinations could carry him above all that. As it was, his self-stereotyping led him away from the work at which he excelled and for which he is important. As he grew older he became less and less a writer of verse and serious non-fiction and more and more a cultural caterer with a hectic schedule of teaching, lecturing and opening exhibitions. Temperamentally, I suppose, he was asking for it. A self-educated man (despite university), he had the self-educated man's lifelong interest in the process of teaching and learning.

What is amazing about *Herbert Read: The Stream and the Source*, this final repayment of old debts, is that Woodcock approaches all Read's fields with equal knowledge and good sense. His discussions of politics as well as of Read's work in art, poetry and the rest, are all well anchored. In a way, this book is more accomplished than those on Orwell and Huxley because the subject is a broader man of letters, a critic seldom content to examine the workings and significance of individual artists or even schools or eras but who rather probed the workings of art and culture themselves and the significance of them in relation to liberty and the quality of life. Read the generalizer was just as much polymath as Woodcock is today, which is one of the reasons this book is so rewarding. It takes one to know one. It takes perhaps a greater one to gain insight into a lesser. The feeling one is left

with is that perhaps only George Woodcock could have done this job so well.
Saturday Night, 1973

ii

The germ of George Woodcock's new book, *Who Killed the British Empire?*, like the germs of many of his other works on history, travel, politics and literature, lies buried in another volume written some time earlier. In this case, the clue can be found in *The British in the Far East*, which he published in 1969. "To many a young Englishman who went East in 1930," he wrote in the introduction to that book, "it must have seemed that the empire would never end, as though the lordly relation in which his race stood to the native peoples of the Far East would continue into the indefinite vagueness of the future." This seed has now grown into a book in which Woodcock traces the ignoble decline of that lordly relation, not just in the Far East but in the whole empire, working backward and forward from the 1930 focal point.

If the question posed in Woodcock's title is partly rhetorical and partly unanswerable, his starting date at least is quite precise. As a result of a few last-minute acquisitions, the empire in 1930 stood at its full height, with a quarter of the world's land surface coloured red by cartographers and a quarter of the world's people sworn to nominal allegiance to the King. The British merchant fleet, despite the devastation of the First World War, was still the largest and most ambitious afloat, and it seemed as though the empire — by now a diplomatic tangle of crown colonies, dominions and almost unofficial dependencies — would go on, in some form, to the end of time.

But if 1930 was the apex of the empire, it was also the beginning of a rapid decline that accelerated after the Second World War. It was a year of events that spelled capitulation and retrenchment. Some of these events, such as Gandhi's famous salt march to Dandi, which stirred the consciousness of India, were apparent at the time. Others were not even clearly identifiable as events, and their importance is seen only in hindsight. It was the year, for instance, marking the beginning of the decade in which Forster, Orwell and an entire breed of anti-imperialist writers came to prominence. It was also a time when small cracks in the system widened and multiplied visibly, at least to those who were looking for them. In Canada, for example, Mackenzie King concluded his first stint as prime minister, having established a policy of creeping independence. The Union Jack, which had followed the traders and merchants, still flew. The military, which had followed in turn the flag, still patrolled in the tropics, in the deserts and even in the Mediterranean.

Woodcock's best books, and his best are very good, have tended to be those in which he brings together not merely intellectual germ cultures but special enthusiasms scattered throughout previous ones. *Anarchism* and *The Crystal Spirit*, his study of George Orwell, were two books it seemed inevitable he would get around to writing. *Who Killed the British Empire?* is another, the product of years of gestation, an even blend of erudition and reason.

Woodcock follows the established pattern of viewing the history of the empire in two phases. The first, the age of the colonies, is brought to an end, following the American Revolution, by the Treaty of Paris in 1783. The second phase, overlapping the other, is the age of imperial mishmash dominated by India and by the white dominions of Canada, Australia and New Zealand. Canada, in fact, plays a decisive role in his account of the disintegration of the empire, an account Woodcock, in his special position as Canadian-citizen-but-world-resident, places squarely in perspective, without regard for either the niceties of Canadian legend (about our role in the War of 1812, for instance) or his own patriotic inclinations.

A long list of names, including those of Gandhi and Franklin Roosevelt, could be shouted in answer to the question of who killed the empire. But such persons were only heralds of a natural attrition, of an idea allowed to fade through a combination of uppishness abroad and growing apathy at home. One great mirror of this transition, and therefore an unindicted co-conspirator in the murder or euthanasia, was Sir John A. Macdonald. By making his famous remark that a British subject he was born and a British subject he would die, while at the same time engineering Confederation and refusing to send troops to the Sudan in 1885, he was illustrating the middle period of empire, wherein allegiance to Britain grew increasingly hollow. The time of unanimous approval of colonialism ended during the eighteenth century. But though the nineteenth century saw radicals in Parliament and in the press, such men, though anti-colonialists, were still pro-imperialists, a distinction Woodcock makes quite clear. Their rise to power marked the beginning of a long period in which it seemed that allowing countries home rule within the empire would be practical and permanent long after colonial domination became distasteful even to Whitehall.

The truth is that the British never really had their hearts in defending their possessions by force of arms: not in the American Revolution, nor in 1812 (when they were too busy fighting Napoleon). Although they put down the Indian Mutiny in 1857, they did not engage in quite the same long, bloody colonial wars the French would later be forced into. The Boer War, the first in which a guerrilla force completely frustrated an army of British regulars, was Britain's Vietnam, and it restated a valuable lesson. Thereafter they were content mainly to make a good show followed by a polite transfer of power, all the while hoping, as even the Fabians hoped, that the past and present colonies would continue to enrich Britain economically.

From the end of the eighteenth century onward, the whole imperial process was one prolonged holding action against a more modern set of beliefs. With the loss of the thirteen American colonies, Britain's attention turned to Canada as the centrepiece of empire. Confederation, and all subsequent persistent affronts to imperial authority, gave heart to India, which was being developed as the third successive base. Eventually the inevitable happened there as well. Britain had little will to resist, what with the economic anaemia brought on by the two world wars and the rise of the United States. The idea of demographic rather than economic imperialism had passed due largely to its very nature. Britain sent more than just men and ships to the colonies; it sent British culture with all that implies. As Woodcock suggests, "One cannot rule indefinitely according to Curzon and teach according to Milton and Shelley."

The usual view of imperial Britain is that, like Rome or Spain in other times, it overextended itself abroad and as a result collapsed at home. There is something to be said for this simple explanation historically, but the issue is much more complex, concerning not so much a British hunger for domination as a British failure to reconcile tradition with progress and a further failure to be equitable about freedom. For most of its tenure, the empire was a bureaucratic nightmare. Some possessions were almost entirely self-governing, others were not self-governing at all. Some were valuable assets in need of constant protection, while St Helena, for instance, was patrolled long after its principal function, serving as the site of Bonaparte's exile, had ended; patrolled just because it was there. One tiny possession, Ascension Island, off the west coast of Africa, didn't even merit the lowly status of colony but was officially HMS *Ascension* and was governed — rather, commanded — like a ship. If the empire was a zoo, it was Orwell's animal farm where all animals were equal but some were more equal than others. It was a messy situation, simpler to let stand rather than to straighten out. Woodcock, in his usual way, has created some order from this diplomatic, economic, geographical and political chaos. Bringing together many of his old subjects with fresh insight and zest, this book is one of his most useful.

Saturday Night, 1975

iii

Two of the recent books by and about John Diefenbaker contain different versions of an anecdote, important only in a broader context, about Gabriel Dumont, the great Métis hunter and leader of Louis Riel's forces in the Saskatchewan uprising of 1885. It seems that around the turn of the century, the Diefenbaker homestead was a stopping-off place for talkative locals and for various strangers to that part of Saskatchewan. Among the visitors were Mounties or former Mounties who were veterans of the battles with the Métis. Another visitor was Dumont himself, whom Diefenbaker remembers meeting and being very impressed with. The year was 1905. Diefenbaker was a precocious ten-year-old. Dumont, at sixty-eight, was one year from the grave.

The meeting is significant, if only symbolically, because it shows one of those curious overlappings of history. There, caught together for a moment in time, was Dumont, who had taken part in the buffalo hunts of another age, and Diefenbaker, who would spend his career in the technological epoch, pining away for that earlier era. There was Dumont, the noble warrior and completely instinctual man; a fellow of great loyalty, courage and wisdom; an illiterate who had no need to be otherwise since he lived by actions instead of by words. There he was meeting Diefenbaker, the heir to his triumphs and follies, who would grow up to live by words alone — great torrents of them — often unsustained by either action or thought. Two ends of the same civilization met that day, two symbols for past and present. It was a third symbol, Riel, who bridged their worlds and set them in perspective. Riel was a man with one foot in Dumont's circle and the other in Diefenbaker's, which is also our own. Unlike Dumont, he became a martyr, and he still comes down to us with a martyr's perpetual timeliness.

George Woodcock begins his biography *Gabriel Dumont, the Métis Chief and his Lost World* with the proposition that though Riel may indeed be the better symbol of the Métis struggle it is Dumont who deserves most of the praise for his military skills and most of the pity for his fate. "It is not Riel we admire," he writes, "for in many ways he was a man impossible to admire, and from all accounts we have, Dumont was a far more likeable and estimable human being. It is Riel the symbol who catches our imaginations and what he symbolises is our inner condition, our consciousness of deprivation and alienation from meaningful existence, our sense of rebellion without hope." True enough, of course. But in another, similarly subconscious sense, we admire Riel for a contrary reason, because part of him is so close to us materially and culturally, whereas Dumont is so remote. It takes Woodcock's considerable narrative and reportorial skills to bring alive the now completely lost world of nomadic hunters and traders.

Unlike Dumont, Riel was well educated and also well rehearsed in the theatrical sense. Despite his racial ties and commitments to the Métis world, he, like the Diefenbakers then in ascent, was conditioned to translate his compassion into mere emotion. It is this fact, I believe, as much as the one Woodcock presents, that accounts for the sweet purgatory of Riel's reputation and also, naturally, for the means of that continued martyrdom: the literary cottage industry that has grown up around his name. Several biographies of Riel have been written over the years. There have also been innumerable articles and essays, several plays (one of them by Woodcock), at least one opera and any number of poem sequences and individual poems, including one by, of all people, Joaquin Miller, the nineteenth century "Byron of Oregon." Even Cecil B. DeMille, in his own kitschy way, had a hand in Riel's legend. In Canada, these past few years especially, the publishing side of

Riel has been an important minor enterprise. The present work is the first substantial one on Dumont; and it is distinguished by the way Woodcock's libertarianism manifests itself as a sort of parapolitical humanism. This allows him to describe "the ordered anarchy" of the hunting expeditions in which Dumont learned the tactics he would use later against Middleton's troops. His premise, of course, is that Dumont is neglected. Also, it is Woodcock's view that Sir John A. Macdonald "seems always to have preferred a devious to a straightforward solution to any political problem." In fact, he thinks Macdonald was something of a scoundrel generally.

This is a fine book, shrewd in its analysis of Dumont particularly and the Métis collectively. It's forceful without being emotional, and it tells what is at times an exciting story. Woodcock has relied upon primary sources. He has also revealed Dumont's personality slowly and in three stages, as though it were a photographic print in the dark-room going through developer, hypo and stopper. The first stage lays the groundwork from his birth in St Boniface, probably in 1837, through his family's return to Saskatchewan. It was there in early adulthood that Dumont showed himself a leader, in the fights against hostile Indians and also against receding prosperity.

The second stage comes with Riel's first rebellion, when Dumont journeyed to Manitoba to offer his services but was largely rebuffed. This precedes Woodcock's canny assessment of the later developments in Saskatchewan:

> For all the rebel leaders with any vision, whether Poundmaker and Big Bear among the Indians, or Dumont and Riel (in his less exalted moments) among the Métis, recognized that the day when they could sweep the white man from the prairies had gone, if it had ever existed. What they hoped was that a strong alliance of the native peoples, willing to take decisive action, could force the Dominion government to negotiate, could assure the Métis a fair position in the new order of the prairies, and could gain the Indians something better than the starvation which by 1883 had in many areas been in result of treaties [with the government] that had cut down the expenditures of the Indian Department on rations at the very time when the full effects of the disappearance of the buffalo were being felt.

The third and most dramatic revelation comes when Dumont's style is contrasted with that of Riel, whom Dumont visited in exile in the United States and helped persuade to return. The fact that he could not further persuade Riel to take his military advice meant the end of any dream of unifying the native peoples. It was this failure to allow Dumont free reign at Duck Lake (where Riel stood among whizzing bullets, holding aloft his crucifix) that made the battle less of a victory than it ought to have been. It wasn't until Fish Creek that Dumont reluctantly went against Riel's scheme. But the move was too late, and resulted in another of those victories that was largely a forestalling of a great inevitable defeat. The defeat, of course, was the defence of Batoche. Following that engagement Riel was captured and subsequently hanged. Dumont, by an even crueller twist of historical fate, fled to the States, where he earned a living performing with Buffalo Bill Cody's Wild West shows.

Had Dumont enforced from the beginning a division of the military and the messianic, the whole Blackfoot Confederacy, plus the English-speaking half-breeds and various other groups, would have joined in one massive and possibly decisive confrontation with the police and militia. Instead, though, Dumont, believing in the power of Riel's charisma (if not fully in Riel's leadership), deferred. The rest is not only history, it's geography.

Woodcock is excellent at the small details that illustrate the differences between the two men and their respective alienation from and hostility towards the enemy. Dumont, for instance, who spoke French and six native languages but hardly any English, always referred to the Canadian soldiers as "policemen" because they wore red tunics similar to those worn by the policemen he had fought in Manitoba. Conversely, Riel, with an astuteness that made him no less a Métis but more of an outsider from the whites, referred to the settlers as "Orangemen." He knew enough of the whites to maintain this fine-line nomenclature; knew them better than Dumont but also knew less how to combat them.

This is a small anecdote, but perhaps it is as symbolic as the one from Diefenbaker's recollections. Dumont was a Métis totally and, as Woodcock states, the greatest leader and hero of his people. Riel, with his seminary training, Eastern clothes and skilful pen, was a Métis in whom the two cultures were more distinct and less in accord. Part of him was native, part was European. Although he tried to align himself completely with the former part, the two halves may have waged within him a war every bit as virulent as that which — foolhardily at times, always sincerely and literally to the last measure of his breath — he waged against the circumstances that had brought about the division in the first place.

There is now a curious irony in the whole situation. Riel became no temporary martyr but rather a posthumous victor. He has become in fact too much a victor, too much a mythological top dog for Woodcock the anarchist and champion of the doomed. By writing this biography Woodcock may have built the foundation on which a rival Métis saint will ultimately be erected, at least in the minds of the whites who are doing all this writing.

Books in Canada, 1976

iv

One title stands out in the current crop of books by George Woodcock because, as well as being a curious volume in itself, it is a useful guide to the other ones. This is *Taking It to the Letter*, a selection of his correspondence with other Canadian writers over the past twenty years. Here as almost nowhere else, one gets a sense of Woodcock as the singular creature he is. Yet at the same time one gets a picture of him as a hard-working, many-sided writer, confronting all the same problems his correspondents do.

We see Woodcock advising young writers, arbitrating feuds, helping friends and offering instruction. We also see him hounded by deadlines, frustrated by publishers and hamstrung by problems with his accounts receivable, just like every other writer. More than ever the book gives us a picture of the persistence that is one of his most admirable traits. Seasons change; children are born, grow up and die; empires fall. Through it all Woodcock tirelessly works away at his books every night, and then, using the journalist's typewriter like Gandhi's spinning wheel, contributes to any periodical or newspaper that wants him. *Taking It to the Letter* gives a view of the workaday writer that's genuinely affecting, as well as insights into how Woodcock decides to publish.

In one letter to a younger writer, for instance, we find him talking about his relatively little-known plays. "Probably my most revealing writings are those which have not yet seen print," he says. These include "a piece of sardonic social criticism entitled *The Benefactor* . . ." Well, *The Benefactor* has finally been published, years after it was broadcast on the radio by the CBC. It turns out to be a satiric portrait of a west coast business tycoon who is not without guile in his charitable impulses. In a preface, Woodcock explains he wrote the play after meeting with a real-life Vancouver mogul who refused to join Woodcock's campaign to aid refugees from Tibet. It shows a rare side of Woodcock, who's usually biting about ideas, not individuals. *The Benefactor* makes me reconsider an old prejudice about the advisability of publishing verse plays which, like old song lyrics, don't often stand the test of print since, by necessity, the verse forms used are more simplistic than those in poetry.

Elsewhere in *Taking It to the Letter*, Woodcock is writing to David Helwig in 1974 about a fragment from a journal that brought Woodcock a lot of comment when it was published in a little magazine. Woodcock reveals that he only sent it to the magazine "with the idea of seeing what the response to it might be and then of getting some idea of whether there was a point in making that kind of writing public." Its reception, he goes on to say, "confirmed my decision to carry on with the memoirs," references to which then recur throughout the rest of the book. Now the memoirs too — or the first volume, *Letters to the Past* — have appeared, and they are altogether remarkable.

For one thing, the book is in a prose far different from that of other Woodcock titles. Normally the consistency of Woodcock's style — within each book and from one book to the next — has been one of his salient features. In *Letters to the Past*, however, he uses many effects. There are numerous individual sentences remarkable for their beauty. One example: "Some of my pleasantest and most poignant memories are of people who never made on history the mark for which they strove." Another one: "About 1930 my Uncle Daffyd Jenkins died of cancer, leaving a vast inheritance of theological texts that in an age of dwindling faith had to be sold by the pound." This second one also gives some hint of the tone of Woodcock's account.

The Woodcocks, it seems, were a family poor in a way not quite genteel. The autobiography is therefore free of stories about hiding from Nanny under the summer porch and going down to Cambridge. Instead, following the death of his father at forty-four, Woodcock was plunged into a dreary life as an obscure clerk in a railway office, from which he emerged about the time of the Second World War. By then he was also thoroughly embroiled in both literary work and radical politics, and had come to the anarchist viewpoint that has sustained him ever since. It was as an anarchist that he refused to serve in the war, and he narrowly escaped prison when many of his friends and colleagues were arrested for sedition. There's quite a lot about Marie Louise Berneri, a member of the same circle and the subject of a remarkable Woodcock poem in his collection *The Mountain Road*. One cannot help but assume that she was probably the great love of his early years, even if Woodcock doesn't actually say so. In any case, the circumspection is atypical of the book, which covers the period up to Woodcock's re-entry into Canada in 1949, for Woodcock here stands naked before his readers.

Historian that he is, Woodcock has also tried to place himself in the context of certain times and places, and the book is a mine of information and anecdote about the British literary and political underground. Generally, he treats old acquaintances most kindly, though there is a reference to "the arch-hypocrite Kingsley Martin," the famous editor of *The New Statesman*, and what seems an unnecessary swipe at the poet and back-to-the-land advocate D.S. Savage, who, unlike Martin, is still alive to read the description. But if I would criticize the book at all, it would be for the way Woodcock is too willing to explain facets of his own character by looking at early events. For instance, he traces his regionalist sympathies to having read as a child histories of Shropshire and Buckinghamshire where he lived. There are perhaps a dozen other examples. But this is quibbling with what is a remarkable autobiography, a story of considerable moral courage and a lifelong progress towards certain educational goals.

Quill & Quire, 1983

THREE

Hugh Garner: A Beginning, a Middle and an End

i

If Hugh Garner were the kind of man who had lived his life among show business personalities he could have written a Hollywood-type autobiography called *Of All People* or *If Memory Serves*. If, conversely, he had passed his time among important events and issues, like the old admirals and statesmen who serialize their memoirs in British Sunday newspapers, he could have called his book *Backward Glances* or merely *Reflections*. As it is, he has found the right title in *One Damn Thing After Another*; for Garner has spent his years stumbling day to day, like the rest of us, through the personal and public hells that make up most ordinary lives. The title also says something about the way in which the book has been put together.

It was in a Bowery flop-house in 1935, when he was twenty-three, that Garner decided to become a writer; and in this memoir he states more than once that his sole original ambition was to produce a good book of short stories, a goal since reached several times. His first publications, however, were articles in *The Canadian Forum*, and during his subsequent career he has vacillated between journalism and fiction, having been, in the 1950s, a prolific magazine writer. Aside from a frequent overlapping of subject matter, the thread that links his work in the two forms is a belief in the old free lancer's maxim — "Waste Nothing." While his stories and to a lesser extent his novels are spare in style, they are rich in small geographical and historical details that seem relevant because they help to create moods. His journalism is likewise littered with eccentric information (though often for its own sake) and tends as well to be repetitious. To the extent, then, that an autobiography should be the distillation of a whole career, this one serves its purpose. As he has always wavered between cheap work and good writing, as though unable to find his right level, so he does in this book, as though unable to decide if his past has been worth the trouble. Little here has been wasted and much has been included that should have been forgotten; and so much from both categories is needlessly repeated that *The Same Damn Things Again and Again* would have been an apt title too.

Garner has written well here, but only in patches, and these invariably are the most revealing of his personality. There is a chunk about his childhood that in a few thousand words puts that period in sharper focus than the whole of his novel *Cabbagetown*. Garner was conceived, he reasons, by accident, and his father kept running out on the family. He spent his earliest years in a back-to-back in Yorkshire, and when the family came to Canada it was natural they should have settled in an Anglo-Saxon slum. The people were poor but proud of being British subjects, the only thing that distinguished them from the other immigrants at whom they looked down their noses. They were staunch conservatives who would have thought no more of considering socialistic solutions to their problems than they would have thought of impugning the King. Garner's link with all this was weakened when he left school at sixteen and got the first of many incidental jobs, as a copy boy on the Toronto *Daily Star*.

That was 1929, the end of Canadian journalism's most storied period, but Garner does not linger on descriptions of the colourful newspapermen as he might have done. As well as being his first address in the suburbs of art, the *Star* was his first glimpse of affluence and power, which in combination with his depressing childhood shaped much of his later thinking. Although he was to fight with the International Brigades during the Spanish Civil War and otherwise mark himself as a leftist, he spends much of the last half of the book explaining exactly how much money he has made from writing and how cleverly. One senses this is brought about not by a late-blooming interest in free enterprise to compensate for years of poverty or even by a subconscious desire to rip off what he could from the exploiters. It seems more a schizophrenic wish to keep intact his proletarian past and at the same time gain acceptance from the Establishment at large or at least its selective representatives.

Here is a man who, he explains, always got on well with such media magnates as Jack Kent Cooke and John Bassett, but whose involvement with less wealthy, less powerful persons in the same business has been an index of friction. Garner reverses the tables by assuming towards the rich the same liberal friendship-at-a-distance attitude some rich assume towards the poor. His is a sort of take-a-millionaire-to-lunch position. Here is a man who got along swell with, even speaks warmly of, Harry C. Hindmarsh (the late *Star* managing editor who is legend for not having practised modern employee relations) but who takes every opportunity to insult Pierre Berton or whoever else constitutes more of a threat by being closer to home.

Garner explains this stance by saying he has always been rebellious towards authority, when actually he has been so only towards selective authority. It is clear, for instance, from the selections on his literary dealings that he thinks all publishers are crooks at heart, rather than the essentially honest semi-competents other writers take them for. His publishers at the moment are Simon & Schuster and McGraw-Hill Ryerson, and he fumes at both of them for being publishers, not merely or specifically for being American-owned ones. Similarly, he fought in the Spanish Civil War and the Second World War to rid the world of Fascism and Nazism but failed to get along with the *immediate* tyranny of officers and the system to the extent that he was jailed in his navy days and once in Spain was actually threatened with a firing squad for having, fittingly, gone over to an anarchist brigade. (It is clear, however, that if he had remained he would have run afoul of the anarchists too.)

It has been much the same with his career, for "writing/publishing, like law, is an adversary occupation" and the fight to get words published, as much as the struggle to get them written, is the immediate war. A great deal of *One Damn Thing After Another* is taken up with his life as a salesman of what he has written rather than as creator of it. Some of this is interesting, such as descriptions of working on a struggling *Saturday Night* and a failing *Liberty*. But mostly it is a ledger of what grudges were held against which editors, how big and frequent the cheques were and how often and when stories were picked up by anthologists and the CBC. He writes hardly at all about himself in artistic terms except to call himself a proletarian, which I suppose he still is, and an anti-intellectual, which he is in the usual but not literal sense. Most of the remarks about his contemporaries are slurs or simple anecdotes. One of the few exceptions is the kind word he has for Morley Callaghan, and this is revealing too. There's Callaghan, a guy ten years older who has been a star ever since Garner was running copy on King Street, an intellectual who writes psychological stuff and therefore would be suspect and probably scorned. But no, Callaghan is all right because he has written about gangsters and ex-cons. Anti-intellectual means dummy, which Garner has never been. He's just an intellectual misanthrope, which makes him fresh and rather appealing.

He has always been first of all a story-teller, in the simple sense, but in this book his own story is none too well related. The work contains all the things for which memoirs are enjoyable but not in the proper combinations or strengths. As for personal anecdotes, there are many good ones, most of them arising from his fondness for drink, which he says the navy instilled in him. There is a complicated story, for example, about commandeering a whore-house while on shore leave in Portugal and, in passing, such gems as the one about getting tossed out of Harry's New York Bar in Paris for fouling its hallowed floor with vomit. But one has the feeling throughout that there is much more he cannot or will not remember.

What is more disturbing, however, is that sometimes bitterness and venom spill from his pen and blot out whatever it was that actually happened. He writes about being interned during the war with so many veiled references and so much hatred that we know the glass house must have been hell. But that's all we know. Was there torture? Were there beatings? All Garner says of the guards is, "I hope God killed them all with cancer." The memories are obviously too painful to be given in detail, and perhaps a good deal of his life has not acquired the distance necessary for dispassionate retelling.

That what he really feels as a writer is also too private must be the reason why he speaks only of "this writing caper." The tone of his remarks is condescending, as though the main market for the book were high-school classes, but this belies a defensive attitude. What he does tell, however, he tells with complete honesty; he has practically no *égoisme dans la fraternité*, only this running paradox about his professionalism as a writer.

At one point Garner states that in his long years as a denizen of rooming-houses he came to know many odd landladies. He then announces he is reprinting in full an old article he wrote about them, and this goes on for several pages. He resorts to such filler many times, and slips in, without credit or warning, as though it were part of the narrative, a piece about hoboing in the Depression that he wrote for *Weekend* and which was later included in Michiel Horn's *Dirty Thirties* anthology. The only time this tactic works at all well (and the only time it is defensible, because the material is nowhere else between covers) is with a series of three articles done in 1959 for the *Star Weekly* about returning to the battlefields of Spain. These moving accounts of how the old *Rojo* tours the turf Franco still holds are interspersed with recollections of the period. This is good history, journalism and travel writing combined, though the ending suffers from appearing to have been stuck on carelessly.

At the end of the book, in the long segment about having sold reprint rights to this and a movie option to that, Garner does two curious things. He talks about how the writing of *One Damn Thing After Another* came about and progressed (it began as a file for McGraw-Hill's promotion department). Then he conducts an imaginary interview with himself in order to work in, before closing, anything he might have forgotten to say. These are strangely boyish tricks but a fitting conclusion to the work as a whole, since throughout Garner has been rather adolescent. He has been bitter and pouting, taking great offense at old affronts others would have dismissed years ago, and he has bubbled like an excited kid about small and medium-sized successes that other writers of his reputation would have been embarrassed to put forward.

When he gives a full account of receiving the Governor General's Award and writes that, aside from first prize in a Charleston contest thirty-five years before, it was the only thing he ever won, we don't know at first whether he is being ironic but then realize, my God, he is not. And when he tells of being interviewed by a critic and having a master's thesis written on his work, we want to squirm with embarrassment for the former slum kid from just west of the Don who still takes every good word as a sign he is overcoming the past he can never forget. When he tells us he titled *Men and Women* (a fine story collection, the realization of his first ambition) as he did because "it was one of those ambiguous titles that might rope in the unwary book-buyer who was furtively seeking a sex manual" — when he does all these things, we think, *For Christ's sake what's going on in this man's mind?* And then at last we know.

"In my sixtieth year," Garner writes, "I sometimes paused and wondered how I'd ever survived . . ." A standard sentiment for survivors like Garner and particularly for those who are loners. Then he goes on and on about rights and permissions, editors' lunches, petty kindnesses and magnanimous insults and the apparent glee with which he barges into publishing houses demanding to see the president. Suddenly, the cumulative effect hitting you like delayed-action vodka, it becomes clear. Hugh Garner, to some very real and very large extent not imagined before, has written eight novels, four books of stories and all the rest, including this autobiographical hodgepodge, because writing is the only surcease for loneliness, and loneliness simple and painful is what his life story has really been about.

Saturday Night, 1973

ii

Hugh Garner's 1950 novel *Cabbagetown*, his second book, has dominated his reputation. It was a straightforward naturalistic story of a young man's progress, away from poverty and towards radicalism, in the 1930s. The book has helped perpetuate the term Cabbagetown, first applied to a small area of southeast Toronto but now taken to mean the whole stretch between Church Street and the Don River. It has also led many people to believe that Garner is a writer primarily concerned with left-wing politics and the 1930s, which he isn't. Certainly it has given many readers the idea that he's basically a writer about the underside of Toronto, which is true only up to a point.

That Garner almost always writes about the present, that he writes about a social sensibility rather than a geographic or political stance, that half of his books have been published in the 1970s — all these facts run contrary to the accepted view that Garner has never quite managed to dispel. An important aspect of his new novel, *The Intruders*, is that he seems to say, "Oh, what the hell, there's no use arguing. I'll give them what they want." On the surface of it, *The Intruders* is a sort of *Cabbagetown Revisited*.

The Cabbagetown Garner knew as a child was full of people just like himself, "the sturdy unkillable infants of the very poor," as the Ezra Pound line has it. It was a labyrinth of rough cottages and brick streets inhabited by immigrants and children of immigrants from England and Scotland. They were the backbone of the Conservative Party, the foundation of royalism, the essence of the Orange Lodge, the bread and butter of the *Evening Telegram*. Like other immigrants, they moved away when they got better jobs, or when their children got them, and as they were gradually assimilated into the mainstream. There was little remorse when, the fashion in slums having changed after the Second World War, some of the streets were pulled down to make way for low-cost government housing. That's the area from which Garner springs, both physically and psychologically. It's also the vantage point from which, in *The Intruders*, he surveys what has become the neighbourhood since his days there.

In the 1970s, TV unit managers, stained-glass artists, lawyers, CBC story editors and other marginal types have purchased old Cabbagetown slums and sand-blasted them, installing skylights and uncomfortable furniture. These are the people and the atmosphere Garner is attacking. Since Garner delights in making the middle class nervous, it's not illogical that he should let himself go and have some fun. And this he does. *The Intruders* at times harks back to the lesser works of Upton Sinclair in being only slightly more a work of fiction that it is a letter-to-the-editor in the form of a novel.

It has the usual run of Garner characters. There's Syd Tedland, a Cabbagetown native of Garner's generation who once conducted a newspaper column but now runs a job printing outfit. There are local winos and miscreants, including a gang of street toughs who, despite the 1970s setting, talk like Huntz Hall of the Bowery Boys. Most importantly, there are idealized members of the honest working class and (to hear Garner tell it) their natural enemies, the twits: "middle class goofballs and artsy-craftsy people looking for a place in what they call 'the inner city.'"

One is a corporate lawyer determined to run for alderman until he sees the light and withdraws to his own end of town. Another professes sociology at York University and calls to mind W.H. Auden's definition of a social worker as one who was put on earth to help the poor but doesn't know what on earth the poor were put here for. One part of the story-line involves street crime. The other concerns the tribulations of a ratepayers' group.

By now, people who care for Garner's work know who they are and those who don't care for it know that they don't and why. This, like all his other books, is a work of realism but not necessarily a realistic book. The writing is of a higher grade than that of the detective novels he's been publishing recently, and there are several fine set pieces. It's significant, however, that nearly all of them deal with Garner-like Tedland, one of the neighbourhood rummies or the police. The real failure of the book, even within the province Garner has established for himself, is that the author deals scathingly and at length with people he does not understand. That's not to say that, if he did comprehend, he would treat them any differently or that he should treat them differently. It's only to say that he tries in *The Intruders*, as in most of his work, to paint a picture through masses of tiny detail but that, in this case, much of the detail is all wrong.

Garner is trying to show that, despite all its protestations to the contrary, Toronto is actually the most class-ridden city on the planet, with the possible exception of Bombay. This is a conclusion hard to disagree with if one is any sort of outsider or from other than the dominant middle class. The way he shows this is not very subtle. He simply lashes out at all the middle class types and their institutions, as though such people *know* that others exist, as though they can be shocked into remembering. Alas, such is not the case in actuality. Toronto looks upon those who aren't middle class Torontonians not as persons apart but as performers hired to entertain them. Attacks always end in frustration, with the villains picking up the heroes' options for another thirteen weeks.

Where Garner really falls down is in dealing with the local political and cultural cabals. The way in which he does so is curious. At times he seems on the verge of turning the book into a *roman à clef*, but just as often he will use the names of actual public personalities. When he does slightly disguise someone, the point is not lost. One of the characters refers to a Ward Seven councilman as "the fruity-voiced alderman that's against everything that makes jobs and helps to build up this city." No one can doubt that the reference is to John Sewell, a reform alderman for that ward who aspires to the working class and is famous for being obstinate.

The Intruders is a grand idea for a Hugh Garner novel but doesn't quite live up to what it promises. The problem is simply that Garner knows more about one side of the tracks than the other. It is interesting to speculate what a writer such as David Lewis Stein, a satirist who knows the ward politicians and cultural bureaucrats, would have done with the same concept. Perhaps he would have excelled at such people while failing with the others whom Garner has depicted rather better. A collaboration would seem unworkable, and it doesn't appear that there exists a proper hybrid, an author who's at once both an insider and an outsider. So it's good that, in view of such a vacuum, we still have Garner, the only important Canadian novelist not from the middle class. He's the only one who, however ineptly at times, can show the other side of the coin.

Saturday Night, 1976

iii

Murder Has Your Number is Garner's fifteenth work of fiction, his fourth crime novel and his third featuring crusty Walter McDumont of the Metro Toronto police. By now certain facts are becoming clear. There is, for example, much less difference between Garner's murder books and his other work than there is, say, between the entertainments and novels of Graham Greene. Sure, the whodunits have so far taken place mostly in small towns and Toronto suburbs (the present one at Yonge and Wilson) whereas the others deal principally with downtown. Naturally there's a difference between a novel that reveals one character in depth and a thriller through which two dozen characters flit. Such matters aside, though, both kinds of books employ similar technique and — significantly — the same social ideas.

Since it's always relied for its realism on a maze of particulars and proper names, the hard-boiled detective story is particularly well suited to Garner, who's written that way regardless of genre. In both the first and third persons, as the case may be, Garner delivers page after page of trivial, phonebookish fact: addresses, street histories, discourses on slang, brand names. Some of it is incorrect but that is all right so long as it sustains the mood. His characters, too, live or die by hard information. The Garneresque hero usually shows sympathy for honest working stiffs by using key words and catch-phrases from their common background. And he slings derisive facts and titbits to express contempt for intellectuals, academics, social climbers, the upper classes as a whole and all those he considers phonies. McDumont, like other Garner top dogs (and like all detective anti-heroes) relishes the cult of the pro. But he shares with GBS the view that the professions are a giant conspiracy against the laity.

In a way all this is more relevant to *Murder Has Your Number* than the actual story-line. Here, as in much of Garner's work, the central theme is class tension, which the plot merely illustrates. A Chinese-Canadian cabby discovers a dead body in the street one night. The corpse turns out to be that of Alan Snelgrove, the inoffensive issue of an Old Ontario Family. He's been shot four times in the face. That the small factory Snelgrove inherited is being picketed by strikers leads to immediate suspicion that labour dissidents are involved. No such luck of course. The cast of suspects McDumont corrals include the victim's mentally unstable wife, her pretentious brother, a shyster lawyer, a sinister accountant and the vulpine lady next door in Snelgrove's ritzy street. In the end, one is surprised by who did it but also by Garner's restraint. He somehow supresses his obvious desire to make all these people equally guilty by reason of their bank-books and educations. Even so, there is sometimes between the lines the suggestion (whether McDumont's or strictly Garner's, it's hard to say) that one Trinity College type killing another is just so much urban renewal.

If all this sounds radical, it shouldn't, at least in any contemporary sense. McDumont (born in Scotland in this book but in *Death in Don Mills* a native Cabbagetowner) comes from what seems another time, an earlier stage of social development. He likes immigrants only when they're struggling; once they've made it, they're poseurs. He's unchangingly hostile to anything smacking of aesthetics or abstract thinking. He has no patience with anyone who exhibits more than a bartender's grasp of psychology.

That's on the minus side. On the plus, he is, without knowing it, a monument to old-fashioned populism. His ideas on class and economic questions have been suggested by his own early poverty, not by a thesis advisor. He still retains some of his grit and his love of simple ways. If at times he lays it on a bit thick, it's usually for a purpose. Above all, he's basically street-wise, not merely up to date on trends in degradation. He's an instinctual man who's smarter than most rationalists. More importantly, he's hip to the class system by which the people who run Canada keep it from being run by anybody else. A preposterously unbelievable character perhaps. But that's the fault of reality, not fiction, least of all Garner's and least of all his books this one, which is subtler than its predecessors but still has plenty of that old Garner sleaze.

Quill & Quire, 1978

iv

With the death in June of Hugh Garner, Canada lost one of its most obstreperous public personalities, most dogged social critics and finest old-style short-story writers. The three roles always seemed to go together, both in his own mind and in the minds of his loyal audience. As this *Hugh Garner Omnibus* helps show, Garner made stories the way a poet makes poetry. He created a great volume of stories over a long period, always shaping and refining, and wrote with such subconscious engagement that, in time, clear patterns and principles began emerging. Sometimes the resemblance of one story to another was purely structural, as in the case of two stories in this collection, "Hunky" and "E Equals MC Squared," which have virtually identical plots. But generally the similarity comes through in another way, as a kind of fictional oneness. That is where the outrageous character and social critic come in.

Much of Garner's reputation still derives from the novel *Cabbagetown*, which is included in this volume in its entirety. It's a good book of its kind (a kind no longer fashionable) but it left many casual readers with the impression that Garner was a bitter trouble-maker from the wrong side of the tracks, a veteran of the Depression who went about recycling his own hard past in fictional form. It's true that his rough life gave him an abundance of good material, which he drew on throughout his career in stories like "Step-'n-'a-'Half," also included here. But he never settled for sprucing up his own experiences. For his past also gave him a sense of the powerlessness of individuals caught up — uncomprehendingly, for the most part — in a social structure in which both access to comfort and the power to change rest with the few and not the many. Garner was always less interested in himself than in other people, and usually the same kinds of people.

In most of the stories and novel excerpts in this book (the last one to appear in his lifetime) the subject is class tension — its destructive effects on society, on human relationships (see "Artsy-Craftsy") and on individuals. To get the message across, he created a stock company of personality types that seemed to appear and reappear, in the best tradition of social naturalism, sometimes with the author's point of view attached to them like baggage labels. But when you take his career as a whole, as this *Omnibus* invites you to do, you find out something else about him: that even when he wasn't writing short stories *per se*, Garner was still a story-teller.

The story-teller is a variety of short-story writer not terribly popular right now but still important to society. The story-teller's tales about human relations are *supposed* to add up to a picture of the social fabric; they're *supposed* to have strong story-lines and plots. The form has always been the choice of many writers who feel acutely, as Garner did, that society leads a life of its own, independent of the people who populate it. In fact, an almost fanatical desire to express this point, to show in intensely human terms how things work, without writing either journalism or historical sketches of the present, has been the hallmark of many otherwise dissimilar writers. It's that quality, for instance, that sets Somerset Maugham apart from Evelyn Waugh and Arnold Bennett from Virginia Woolf and John O'Hara from John Updike. Now by most criteria one must classify the Waughs, Woolfs and Updikes as "better," deeper, more stylish writers. But that's not really the point when you consider that they have a different mission. Defined in such terms, Garner had few serious rivals as Canada's journeyman story-teller (as distinct from maker of literature). Certainly there seems no one willing to replace him. He stood all alone, and this book, despite obvious and major flaws, is a kind of memorial.

Canadian Reader, 1979

FOUR:

Louie, Ezra and Everybody Else — A Primer

In 1949 the Montreal poet Louis Dudek wrote a letter to Ezra Pound, then in his sixty-fourth year, praising Pound's life-work, the tortuous, haunting *Cantos*. Dudek was thirty-one at the time and living in New York, holding down a small teaching job at CCNY while working on his Ph.D. at Columbia. His letter was the common, respectful kind from a young poet to a great, ancient one, and perhaps he did not even expect a reply. But soon an envelope arrived from the Washington, D.C., mental hospital where Pound had been remanded indefinitely after being declared unfit to stand trial for treason. Soon there developed a full-blown correspondence between the two writers and also a curious, ultimately sad relationship that would have great effect on the future of poetry in Canada. It is an unusual and engaging story that comes to light now, with the publication by Dudek, himself now something of a grand old man, of *Dk/ Some Letters of Ezra Pound*.

Pound's seventy letters, postcards and telegrams to Dudek, reproduced in facsimile with copious notes by the recipient, cover the period to 1967, five years before Pound's death, with the heaviest concentration coming in the early 1950s. As it gives insight into the sender, the collection is useful in two ways. First, it shows us over a long period Pound's relationship with one man and what's more important with a younger, relatively unknown man. While *Pound/Joyce*, the correspondence between Pound and James Joyce collected in 1968, was also limited in scope to two persons, it was concerned mainly with two titans, one of whom (Pound) was forever trying to lecture the other as a peer. It was, of necessity, distorted. Second, the present book brings the reader relatively up to date. While D.D. Paige's standard edition, *The Letters of Ezra Pound*, was useful in showing a diversity of relationships, it stopped in 1941, long before Pound began broadcasting over Mussolini's radio network and long before his sanity was called into question. The Dudek correspondence, by contrast, shows an old man who believed (not always without cause) that he was being persecuted, dealing freely with one whom he had reason neither to put down nor to promote. It is as close to a one to one relationship as Pound ever seems to have become involved in. So this look at the private Pound is useful as a literary historical document but also as a possible aid in answering the big questions: Was Pound a racist? Was he senile? Was he truly crazy?

Dudek doesn't exert himself answering these questions, and the reader is left to reconfirm whatever views he has held all along. What Dudek does underscore clearly is that, all else he might have been, Pound was certainly a crank. It's not difficult to see why, since he falls into such a recognizable pattern, one not altogether unfamiliar with literary genius.

Pound was a man who spent a lifetime trying to convince himself that he wasn't really from Hailey, Idaho, where, though he had been born there never to return, his intellectual roots, in the direct sense of that phrase, remained for all his eighty-seven years. He came out of that energetic tradition of American populism, a political tradition that Pound, an artist instead of a politician, strove to transfer to his own discipline. He was a product of the West when the West was farther west than it had been a few generations before, but this made little difference to the line of descent. He resembled Aaron Burr and Andrew Jackson, those long-lived individualists reeking of charlatanism, with *Blackstone's Commentaries* in one hand and duelling pistols in the other. He was, in short, a hell-raiser and a mover and shaker, but different from his antecedents in important ways.

For one thing (though it seems strange to say), he tired easily. With acknowledged help from T.E. Hulme and F.S. Flint and unacknowledged help from Sadakichi Hartmann, Pound chiselled in stone the precepts of the imagist movement and thereby changed the entire course of English language poetry, in fact of literature as a whole. Although he continued to pick out and teach the best of each succeeding generation — one thinks immediately of Eliot, Lawrence, Hemingway; even of Dudek, a far more important poet than he's sometimes given credit for being — there were always, in the background, pretensions that muddled his thinking; pretensions born of the climate from which he came.

As Burr and Jackson were lawyers who used their knowledge as a stepping-stone to military and political careers, so Pound was a writer who used his talent as a stepping-stone to some sort of public life, the desire for which was always at odds with his need to create. When he got Hemingway's generation on what he considered the proper track, he retired to Italy in 1924 to devote himself to his own writing, though not to the exclusion of other people's. Although it was during this period that he fashioned some of his most difficult verse, he found that even this accomplishment fulfilled neither his ambitions nor his pretensions. He learned the sad truth that a writer's most powerful place in society is as no writer at all but as a sort of wholesaler of opinions, esoterica and general ideas. The first two Pound never had any diffiuculty supplying on demand. He was, after all, a gregarious mediaevalist and a tinker with languages, even ones remote from his own. But the third commodity always gave him difficulty and led to what, I think in fairness, can still be called his downfall, even if it was also his literary martyrdom.

Pound apparently was not a dangerous bigot but he came from a place and a time in which to call someone a wop or a kike was nothing to feel guilty about. The gap between formal English and conversational English was wider perhaps than ours is today, and slurs of this kind were merely part of natty conversation. They showed, he believed, that he was a man of the world, a man of public affairs: something he dearly wanted to be, sometimes more than he wanted to be a poet. This explains, for instance, his professed authority in (and genuine knowledge of) music, which he thought broadened him, this Idahoan, and made him more *public*. It may also explain the unequal ratio of expounding on and dabbling in economics and politics, which brought such calumny down on him and culminated in the *Pisan Cantos* but also in his twelve-year confinement to St Elizabeths Hospital. And this is where Dudek comes in.

Dudek wasn't expecting to carry on a long correspondence. Neither was he expecting to be conscripted into Pound's literary army in exile. Still, when that took place he was pleased to oblige the master, at least for a time, however distasteful the obligation sometimes was. Dudek wanted to debate poetry and ideas with Pound but Pound was interested mainly in making a convert. Dudek sent Pound a few of his poems and later, back in Montreal, some of the Canadian literary periodicals of the day. Pound almost from the first sent Dudek various European magazines and newspapers relating to whatever current social theories he claimed to have formulated in response to the shabby state of world affairs. From the first he also sent Dudek the names and addresses of people he thought the younger man should meet. Some of them Dudek disregarded. Other people he looked up, and in this way formed important friendships with poets such as Paul Blackburn and Cid Corman.

In his notes, Dudek recalls his distress at realizing that for Pound "propaganda for his ideas had become more important than literary value" and that Pound was "unwilling to go into objective details, but very quick on the draw for general invective." Here was Dudek, a young intellectual loose on the big world for the first time, eager to argue and to learn. And here was Pound, tired and old and more than a little bitter; still uncanny in discovering new writers but more interested now in social theories which he thought might restore him to grace and of which this time he could be the central figure instead of a discoverer and critic.

Being the type of American he was, a triumph of energy and intellect over reason and understanding, Pound was naturally a conspiracy buff, and one wonders what he thought of the assassinations of Martin Luther King and the two Kennedys, all of which he lived to see from afar once repatriated to Italy in 1958. As it was, he had passed through periods of interest in Social Credit and Gesellism and came, by the time Dudek entered the picture, to believe that world politics had long been manipulated by a mysterious group of international financiers. Although there is something to be said for his theory of debit financing among Western nations, Pound bore approximately the same relation to the serious economists' ideas as Steve McQueen bore to Stanislavsky's ideas about acting. He not only believed in the existence of the gnomes of Zürich, he tended to believe that they were Jewish gnomes. This led to some strange revelations in these letters to Dudek, including some that Pound ordered deleted before publication.

Pound was forever suggesting books for Dudek to read. One of them was *Mein Kampf*, the thought of which Dudek found repugnant. Pound made clear that while he himself was never a subscriber to Hitler's views, only to Mussolini's, he believed Hitler's autobiography an unjustly maligned piece of work. Pound also asked Dudek to purchase, read himself and then send to St Elizabeths everything he could find by Alexander Del Mar, an eccentric American economist and historian. He was also eager to obtain a work interpreting the murder of Abraham Lincoln in terms of a world-wide monetary conspiracy. Dudek dutifully passed on what he could and read almost everything suggested to him (including some of Mussolini's writings) but was not much impressed. He even went to visit the old man in hospital. He includes here a moving account of that meeting, as well as the script Dudek prepared for CBC-Radio on Pound's letters to other people, which Pound said he enjoyed.

The reason for the deterioration of the relationship was the involvement of Dudek, one of hundreds of writers around the world who tried to help Pound, in attempting to spring the old poet from hospital. Part of the involvement with this cause was a piece Dudek printed in a little magazine he was editing, which happened to mention the fact that Pound carried on a voluminous correspondence from St Elizabeths. Pound thought it would prejudice his case, such as it was, to have it known that he was in contact with a great many persons on the outside. The friendship cooled.

Dudek, who had only the best intentions, apparently thinks this reaction was paranoia on Pound's part. It may or may not have been. Certainly there is a tendency for Canadians to think Americans are paranoid about U.S. parapolitics, when in fact the Americans are often vindicated later by revelations of new shenanigans in high places. Whatever the truth in this case, the letters were much less frequent from that point on. The correspondence ends with Pound's last-minute refusal, because of failing health, of an invitation to a world poetry conference Dudek was helping organize as part of Expo 67. The immense impact Pound had on Dudek as a poet was established long before the breakdown of the personal relationship, and it continues even now, with noticeable effect on Canadian poetry.

Although he may have been undirected in literature, just as he was in other fields, Pound was foremost the man who took poetry away from nineteenth-century formalism, with its imposition of strict form on content and emotion, and spun it around towards imagism, fresher imagery, looser metrics and a vaguely Oriental sparseness. That is mainly why Dudek was interested in him, and that is mainly why he tried to listen to him and assist him and why, even now, in the running notes to this book, he defends Pound's use of ethnic and racial slurs in these letters. Such involvement would be less important than it is had not Dudek's help spread Pound's poetic influence throughout Canada, where for better or worse it is very much alive today.

By the time this exchange began Dudek had already edited with Irving Layton the magazine *First Statement*, a literary journal dedicated to what was new in Canadian poetry. What was new was principally the poetic diction of Pound and Pound's friend William Carlos Williams. When Dudek returned to Canada he helped edit another magazine, *CIV/n* (the title from one of Pound's letters), and also joined Layton, Raymond Souster and, later, Peter Miller in running Contact Press, which published mostly collections by younger poets. It is not so much that these Canadian writers imposed themselves on their contemporaries as that they did what Pound had done in England and America: they changed things around. The main thrust of Canadian poetry in English would not always be obviously connected with Dudek's Poundism and Souster's Williamsism, but it would henceforth be much different from what it had been before they came along.

Pound wisely had abandoned the imagists as a group when he saw them growing stale, though by then their changes had already been wrought. In Canada the transition was not so rapid or the results so clear-cut. Dudek states rightly that Pound "has not been sufficiently recognized" as the father of the Black Mountain school of poetry, whose Canadian adherents were those connected with the Vancouver magazine *Tish* in the early 1960s and, later, the Coach House Press in Toronto. Between this group and the poets more attuned to Dudek there have been many skirmishes. Viewed in historical terms such battles have been merely the dog attacking its own tail, and today there is little opposition left to the poetical causes of Pound. Such squabbles as take place are between people whose main disagreement is in outlook rather than technique. That what today is freshest and most popular in our poetry goes back to Pound, the Pound Dudek sought out initially, is not difficult to prove. An arbitrary chronology shows how it worked, and shows the importance as a document of *Dk/ Some Letters of Ezra Pound*.

Before the First World War, Pound, with his love of Whitman and his disdain of the formalist Americans since Whitman's time who cultivated a British style, first publishes the imagists as a group, carefully including both young English as well as American poets. This influences Williams, who in the 1940s begins to influence both Souster and Layton and the incipient American Beats. Williams writes a letter encouraging Souster and writes an introduction to one of the early books of Layton. Dudek's relationship with Pound is still afloat. Back in Canada, Dudek starts Contact Press with Souster and Layton. Among the books published is Dudek's *Laughing Stalks*, in which the poet makes mild fun of some of his contemporaries. Also included are the first full-length collections of George Bowering, Leonard Cohen and Margaret Atwood. Bowering becomes involved in the *Tish* group on the west coast, Cohen names Layton his mentor and Atwood becomes increasingly imagistic, at length perfecting a style midway between the old avant-garde and the Black Mountaineers.

Aside from her and aside from Souster, who is still revered by a number of *Tish* people who have come east and become involved in Coach House, there is now a clear split between those who adhere to Pound-Williams imagism and those who adhere to Black Mountain imagism, both of which have roots in the United States, the latter more recently. The British for their part have meanwhile forgotten what they've learned and gone back to writing like Matthew Arnold.

The older poets write about their weariness with the world, as did Pound and others who lived through the First World War. The Beats write the same way but also write about their private and public joys as residents of a planet doomed by the cold war. The *Tish*–Coach House–Black Mountaineers reject world-weariness and also the Beats' duality of attitude. Allen Ginsberg, the head Beat, pays homage to Pound. Coincidentally he is courted by some of the *Tish* veterans. He is also published by Dennis Lee at House of Anansi, which has republished Margaret Atwood's early Contact book.

Lee leaves Anansi and Margaret Atwood is one of those active in his place. She publishes George Bowering. Dudek publishes his own *Collected Poetry* and is given a bad review by Lee. Bowering publishes a book called *Curious* with Coach House in which he attacks Dudek and Layton and kids a bit with Souster and Atwood. Meanwhile, Pound dies and Leonard Cohen becomes a recording star about five years too late. Also about this time Bowering wins a Governor General's Award and is criticized for his American influences. The fuss refers to his link with Black Mountain rather than his more indirect one with Pound, who is now so far in the past as to be respectable: like United Empire Loyalist blood.

None of the above is quite so facetious as it sounds, though of course it is far from a balanced view. It is only by way of showing that Pound — the serious Pound of his own poetry and the crank Pound of these letters — is one of the fathers of it all, which makes this fascinating book all the more important.

Saturday Night, 1975

FIVE

Poetry Chronicle

i

In one of those meltings of language that are always taking place, the phrases "collected poems" and "selected poems" are growing to mean much the same thing. In times past when a poet published a collected volume it meant that he was dead or very nearly so, and that the book contained, with perhaps only a few exceptions, every verse he had ever published. He felt no shame in collecting them all because, not having had to publish or perish or make a name while still young, he wisely had refrained from printing in the first place those he knew would not stand up. There were no such things as a Collected Early Poems or a Collected Shorter Poems; the phrase was applied to a person's life-work. Conversely the term "selected poems" did not have about it the finality it is now beginning to assume. It was used by living poets to bring together the best of their stuff that was out of print in order to allow them to proceed, to go on to larger and better things, safe in the knowledge that their pasts were uncluttered. It is indicative of Ralph Gustafson — a clearly modern poet with a rare sense of the continuity of things — that he should have maintained this fine line syntax. His *Selected Poems* is a sorting out, an updating, a housekeeping job. Already he has changed directions and pushed on ahead with a little volume entitled *Theme and Variations for Sounding Brass*.

Gustafson is a figure it would be difficult to imagine springing up in the North or western Canada, where there remain vestiges of the frontier life-view, for he is one of those Quebec poets who, like A.J.M. Smith, John Glassco and F.R. Scott, has gathered from that older section of the country an awareness of not only his own history but of past lives and old cultures generally. At this point, however, except for flashes of the part of his own wit that resembles Scott's, the lumping together must end, because of the extremity of Gustafson's historical sense. Who else, for example, could honestly state in a poem that while flying at 13,000 feet over the Yukon his thoughts naturally turned to da Vinci, Cayley, Santos and Wright and the evolution of human knowledge making possible the invention of the aeroplane? Cultured is the word for what he is, though as one born when he was (Gustafson is sixty-three) he is, like it or not, for better or worse, a thoroughly modern man; and it is evident this dichotomy causes within him a constant tension. A great many of the more than 100 poems reprinted here arose from his travels in the Old World — Egypt, Greece, Italy, Britain and Spain — and at times one thinks he is removed mentally from contemporary North American society except insofar as it is, alternately, a ruin of or a monument to the civilizations for which the Atlantic was a one-sided ocean. But then in the middle of it all he writes that he is in fact aware of this and in no small way disturbed by it:

Four thousand saints surround me.
My soul is utterly taken by the man
Selling Cokes from a red refrigerator
On the roof of Milan Cathedral.

I am unused to this commercial society
And walk the lead slope near the balustrade
With mine eyes as if they did not see
The solid wooden booth and the counter

But it is no use: the sun broils
And the cathedral is a million dollar failure.
The Virgin Mary and Christ holding
Open like a miraculous cardiac his bleeding

Heart, are for sale in coloured plaster. . . .

It becomes clear, in fact, that the modern self is winning the struggle. Although he published his first book in 1935 and two others during the first years of the war, Gustafson has included in this collection, with two exceptions, nothing earlier than poetry from *Flight Into Darkness* (1944), meaning that he has chosen not to reprint the sonnets and traditional lyrics that gave him his early international reputation. In the patterns of those poems he has included, which are arranged more or less chronologically, it is easy to see that the poet is in a way growing younger, in outlook and method. To observe the latter shift at its simplest it is necessary only to thumb through the book, noting at the front the curiously modern (perhaps at times even trendy) line breaks and, at the back, despite the continued tone of sophistication, the poems so thoroughly contemporary that one can squint, look at their arrangements on the pages and know that they are modern poetry.

But these are stylistic occurrences. The manifestation of the tug of war between the two Gustafsons is *Theme and Variations for Sounding Brass*. Though here too the voice speaking to the reader is that of continued education and inherited cultures (the title in some small way reflects his interest in music, on which subject he conducts a CBC radio programme), the five longer poems are a confrontation with the current events and the violence which, though part of the nature of the beast, cannot help but appal men of conscience. "Nocturne: Prague 1968," as moving a poem as written in Canada, is an anguished denial of politics, and "Fanatasia on Four Deaths," about the Kent State massacre, is partially made up of "found" statements by Spiro Agnew in order to show their mindlessness as much as to mock them. Between the middle poem and the fifth and last one, which concerns the further cheapening of life through televised reports of mass death, is "Aubade: Quebec," an eloquent response to the Laporte murder, a sort of poem for voices including his own, which alarms him as it becomes complacent or at least compassionate out of some sense of duty. As the book concludes: "The trouble is there is too/Much death for compassion." *Theme and Variations for Sounding Brass* is the work of a poet who bridges the gap between aesthetics and the daily news, who combines a knowledge of all that has happened before with a belief that it should not continue unchallenged.

Saturday Night, 1972

ii

It has now been ten years since the Periwinkle Press in Vancouver brought out John Newlove's first major (and now scarce) poetry collection, *Elephants Mothers & Others*, at a time when there were many obviously important poets in their early and mid-twenties. In fact, what with Newlove, Atwood, MacEwen, Bowering and the rest, there were probably more ripening then than now. But what in retrospect seems remarkable — in light of the Zieroths and Musgraves and Flanagans — is that so many of them had, and still have, so much in common. As diverse as their chosen directions sometimes seem, they all wrote and continue to write on pretty much the same principles and with basically the same intent. With few exceptions they share a tone of detachment they have perfected and intensified in wildly different ways while still keeping their common lineage clear. Perhaps it is because the modernist tradition from which they derived now seems to be wearing thin that the new poets, groping, seem less a group. Whatever the case, the 1960s poets I speak of sometimes seem like a Siamese chorus line, all the members kicking in different directions but each one joined to the next. The one who is kicking highest, at himself — and this is a recent development — is John Newlove.

In his new collection, *Lies*, one sees a sharp break from his other books. Where once he wrote largely outside himself, he now is very contemplative, in a somehow violent sort of way; and where once his poetry was explosive it is now implosive, going deeper into its own structures as the poet goes deeper within himself. The change from even *The Cave*, published in 1970, is striking. In that collection, more so than in the earlier *Black Night Window* but in a clear progression nonetheless, he was concerned with poetic neatness and had an understated epigrammatic quality he now seems to be throwing away. The sixty-five or so new poems in *Lies* are starker by reason of the roughness of their revelations and are, in general, tougher, harder, more against the grain — and this from a poet who was never in the first place dull-edged, meek or pussy-cattish in the least. Technically the effect is that the poems are more fragmented and disjointed than earlier ones, but more accomplished. The poems seem to be wrung from the mind, dripping on the pages, and when they work they work powerfully indeed.

But *Lies* is not all plumbing the ullage, but is the result of a tension between, on the one hand, the struggle against the inarticulation all poets must face, and, on the other, the desire to bring back something from the Other Side, to return to the conscious with, in clear form, what in the subconscious is merely code. The dilemma is common enough; the difference here is that Newlove does it better than most, and the result causes a pain that rings horribly true. And yet all the poetry in the book is not essentially this indoor poetry. Newlove still writes openly about what have become his recognizable themes. The cruelly ironic love poetry, the poetry of the derelict, the poetry about the haunting purity of the Indians — it is all still there, along with found poetry and translations. But what remains the most effective is the poetry about other people's and by implication Newlove's hopelessness.

Books in Canada, 1972

iii

Often the reviewer's tendency, for the sake of convenience, is to think in terms of generations, of writers the same age who therefore must have something in common; and to put aside, because they are complicated, the environmental and educational factors that split generations into much smaller groups. Any idea, for instance, of a cohesive lot of sixtyish Canadian novelists shaped by the Depression and the two world wars is shot to hell if one considers that Hugh Garner and Robertson Davies were born only six months apart. There is a similar danger in thinking of Dorothy Livesay as mainly a 1930s poet, for though much of what she wrote in that decade may strike us now as typical stuff of the day, she has — more than most writers her age — consistently moved off in other directions since then, in the same way she moved into proletarian poetry only after working elsewhere. All this can be seen clearly in her *Collected Poems: The Two Seasons*, a choice of nearly 300 poems spanning almost fifty years.

The book is made up of eighteen sections, with the earliest poems dated 1926. The final section is a poem sequence, "Disasters of the Sun," written in 1971. She has included many hitherto unpublished poems, slipping them in among the selections from her ten or so previous books, more or less chronologically in order of composition. The overall effect is one of steadily increasing energy and health, like the hospital chart of a patient who started out near death and grew progressively stronger and, in a way, younger. Also, there are noticeable shifts in the tone of the poems, with the earliest ones, generally simple lyrics and rhymes of love and nature, in a different voice from the Marxist poetry of the 1930s, the documentary poetry of the 1940s and the contemplative, descriptive and love poetry of the 1950s and after.

Most of the poems representing her teens and twenties are pleasant enough and usually traditionally metric, though they become harsher and less measured as they go. Some poems, though decidedly happy in intent, can sound to the contemporary ear like something spoken by Chief Dan George:

My joy knows no house
It is too wide
For any walls to measure it.
The leaping sun
The flying grass
Can be its only boundary . . .

Following the earliest poems is a sort of transitional group, similar to the first, in which the poems become longer, more intricate and generally more ambitious, and come to a climax in the section "The Thirties" and in particular in the long narrative poem "In Green Solariums," about a prostitute who acquires a social conscience and marches with the workers. If that seems a little melodramatic by current standards, it works as well aloud, slowly, now as it probably did then and gives one some small faith in a Canadian radical tradition too often despaired of as not going back far enough or as having wide gaps in its lifeline.

But there is in this section one poem which, though not representative of Dorothy Livesay's sometimes beautifully bleak 1930s poetry, can be held up as something of a statement on the time. In "Comrade" the speaker recalls the man who deflowered her, his "hands were firm upon me: without fear / I lay arrested in a still delight — / Till suddenly the fountain in me woke." Which, poetically, is nothing out of the ordinary. But in the second stanza she sees the old lover years later "a grey man without dreams, / Without a living, or an overcoat" and claims that in that situation, in solidarity against the capitalist oppressors, "we are more close / Than if our bodies still were sealed in love." She also gives expression to a few sensible enough emotions which, though not political, are just as dated. In one poem, for instance, she speaks pityingly of an immigrant in Montreal, something one could scarcely imagine a Canadian poet doing today.

In the 1940s Dorothy Livesay wrote her documentaries, long verse plays or poems for voices drawn from history, as in the 1945 poem about Riel, "Prophet of the New World," or from recent events, such as "Call My People Home," about the internment of Japanese-Canadians in British Columbia during the Second World War. During that period she was also writing some of her best shorter poems, though the 1950s, which saw the publication of her *Selected Poems*, was on the basis of its representation here a more prolific decade. Yet her better work, that of the 1960s, is given the most play and includes a series of poems done in Britain; the poems arising from her UNESCO teaching experience in what is now Zambia; and the sophisticated erotic poetry of *The Unquiet Bed*, a remarkable book she selects from generously. Those are followed by about forty poems from both editions of *Plainsongs* (books not widely enough circulated in their original forms) and a small bit of still more recent poetry.

Collected Poems: The Two Seasons has apparently caused Dorothy Livesay to consider her work as a whole, for generally speaking she has kept fewer of the early poems than in her *Selected Poems* of fifteen years ago. Throughout the book the sections become longer as the poet seeks and then loses all the polemic and is influenced by and then discards various British models, and as the poems themselves become meatier. In the second half of the book there is much that could be quoted, though here is a poem for her husband that shows the volume is not only an important document on the evolution of Canadian poetry but also, to a large extent, a living book, far beyond any archival importance. It is called "The Incendiary":

Now that the poetry's bursting out
all over the place
firecrackers setting off explosions
under train wheels
bombs
under hydrants
"bloody marvellous"
I can hear you saying
your eyes bulging and blazing
with that flinty excitement

as if every bone in your body
though burnt now   to ashes
had started a conflagration
had gone off crackling
and shooting poems
all over the bloody map
Canada —

country you came to, late
and loved with hate
and longed to set fire to. . . .

Saturday Night, 1973

iv

In his preface to a recent collection of York University student poetry, Irving Layton hit upon something true and wise when he listed what he considers the four main groups in English-Canadian poetry today. The first two groups, he said, are the Indians and the Loyalists — WASPs differing mainly in the swiftness of their rejection of the United States. As examples, he gave Dorothy Livesay, Dennis Lee, Al Purdy. Next were what he called the Frygians, or disciples of Northrop Frye, whose most distinctive features are a love of myth and a belief in the dominance of the imagination. Finally, Layton wrote, there are the Jews, the cosmopolitan and generally urban poets. In giving examples of each, Layton listed the early Eli Mandel, the one we see a lot of in *Crusoe: Poems Selected and New*, as a Frygian, along with such obvious examples as Jay Macpherson and James Reaney. But he cited the more recent Mandel, that of his other new book, *Stony Plain*, as belonging to the urban Jews. Some argument could be made for the more political, topical and landscape-conscious Mandel of *Stony Plain* being at times a Loyalist too. The conclusion to be drawn from this is that Mandel is a poet with traditions coming out his ears and that *Stony Plain* is an attempt to come to terms with them, though the changes probably will be fully realized only in another collection sometime in the future.

The seventy-five or so poems in *Crusoe* are taken from *Stony Plain* and from four earlier books, ranging from *Trio* (in which Mandel shared space with Gael Turnbull and Phyllis Webb), published in 1954, to *An Idiot Joy*, for which he received a Governor General's Award in 1967. The selection was made by Margaret Atwood and Dennis Lee, to whom the book is dedicated. Just why the choice was not Mandel's own is a mystery; a selected edition of a living poet made by other than the author himself is seldom defensible unless the writer is a critical dunce, which Mandel, as the author of two critical books and editor or co-editor of six anthologies, is not. They have done a creditable job, however, rarely sacrificing the best individual poems for the most representative, or vice versa. Their apparent aim was to show a clear but smooth change from Frygianism to near-Loyalism, popism almost, without adhering to strict chronology, and in this they have succeeded.

There are several things included in the selected poems to represent the period when Mandel was involved with turning myth to contemporary account, such as the second of the "Minotaur Poems" from *Trio*, in which the speaker's father, an incessant tinker in his garage, is revealed at the end as Icarus falling from the sky in homespun wings. Here as in most of the poems there is a sheer doggedness of language — a nearly physical repulsion at the *almost* right word — that is the most noteworthy characteristic of Mandel's technique and which he manages to retain even when working a more recent vein seemingly opposed to it. Sometimes the way he maintains the precision is by reverting to epigrammatic poetry, the use of which is sometimes a mark of the Loyalists, whom Mandel also resembles in his historical awareness, one that occasionally transforms itself into popism, as in many of the poems in *Stony Plain*.

These are Mandel's most interesting work. They are also his most accomplished, since he drops his formal position as recycler of myth and champion of the imagination and writes more from the gut, while retaining his authoritative diction. When he writes of personal anguish, it is anguish clear and simple, forcefully conveyed. Always an intensely intellectual poet, he continues to be one in the *Stony Plain* poems while leaving his shell and taking part in the day to day world, his concern for which previously was pretty well limited to painful memories of his Depression childhood.

The poems in *Crusoe*, excepting the new ones, use myth not in a classical way but as source material for all that is miraculous and strange. If an interest in the occult it be, it is an interest in the occult as anthropology and intellectual exercise: he is not so much like Poe as like Lafcadio Hearn. Perhaps the principal difference between these poems and the new ones from *Stony Plain* is that Mandel now takes myth where he can find it, and he finds it particularly in the popular hero of the amorphous Left. Throughout the new book there are poems in memory of this person and that, as though the obituary columns have taken for him the place once held by *The Golden Bough*. Among those whose passings have stirred him are Camus and the poets A.M. Klein and John Berryman. This partly illustrates Mandel's new role as man of awareness in the contemporary world. An even better illustration is his poem for Jimi Hendrix and Janis Joplin, though it falls apart at the end in a giant fragmentation that is the chief threat to his new-found strength. Somewhere near the middle of the poem, he writes:

> *I loved you Janis*
> *as I love those whom terror seized*
> *for its own poetry: Roethke and Agee*
> *Dylan, Crane, Jarrell, and Sylvia*
> *dead at last in the oven of her own head*

That's concise emotion one would not have heard from Mandel before, though the touch of the indoorsman — the honour roll of poets — is indicative of the way he formerly worked. Emotions reminded him not of other emotions but of poets or painters or film-makers, or the other way around. Hence in other poems we have Goya, Rembrandt and Grosz, Alex Colville and Jack Chambers. Not surprisingly, however, these last two occur in the ultra-realistic newer poems devoid of Old World gesturing, the loss of which he has balanced with a new interest in politics, both Loyalist anti-American and Jewish internationalist. At times these poems veer towards the trendy, but thankfully they are free from cries of solidarity.

Saturday Night, 1973

V

Something reviewers ought never do is either praise or damn a book's jacket blurbs, as though their existence were somehow the author's fault. Another act to be avoided is cheating the writer and the audience by reviewing the author's photograph, but in the case of Joe Rosenblatt's seventh book, *Dream Craters*, this last punctilio can be ignored. This new collection of Rosenblatt's poetry, selected by John Newlove, has no blurb but something much better: a picture that says it all about Rosenblatt's poetic persona. It's a grainy, black and white, frontal head-and-shoulders shot of the poet as free-lance pixie and wrestler with chaos in the modern world. His sweater doesn't fit, his necktie's askew and his collar bent, and his hair protrudes from either side like sharp spokes, but his deportment is bravely erect, his eyes surprisingly clear and his mouth formed in a sort of beatific snigger. It's beautiful, it's pure Rosenblatt, it's exactly like his poems.

Fortunately this is a fairly big collection, for his poems have to be taken in large doses. He seldom writes remarkable individual poems that anyone could call surprisingly good or surprisingly bad. Instead he has been writing for years one long discontinuous poem about the emotional state of himself and his fellows and about the dangers of Christian Science in matters of mental health. He does what almost no one else does and he does it well and makes it funny.

Something of a poetical hypochondriac, Rosenblatt elevates his depressions into fantasy by beginning with the lyrical and stretching it into the absurd. His tools are metaphor and simile, and these come in two kinds. One is the type used by Peter De Vries that's so precise and fresh it makes you stop to appreciate it. The other variety is like something from Richard Brautigan. It confounds the reader with its incongruity ("My spirit is an invisible chauffeur . . .") but, when you begin to ponder it, becomes doubly appropriate in the context of Rosenblatt's delightful mind.

Part of the fun is eavesdropping on Rosenblatt's word-play. He relishes arcane words and uses them correctly, though for no other apparent reason than that they are interesting words. His emotions are like that too, a cross between the eccentric and the slapstick; and he bears a striking resemblance to Gregory Corso, mainly insofar as Corso too owes his strongest allegiance to the unlikely duo of Shelley and Mack Sennett.

Many of Rosenblatt's earlier and perhaps best-known poems were those in *The LSD Leacock* and *Winter of the Luna Moth* celebrating and contemplating various animals, fishes and eggs. In *Dream Craters* there is only one such poem, "Mandrill Baboon," the inclusion of which it's tempting to call atavistic. What the book consists of mostly is poetry arising from the introspection forced upon him by the shabby state of the world. Plastic decadence causes him to brood (in the nineteenth century he would have belonged to the laudanum school) but it is a brooding that turns to comedy.

It also causes him, in "Sleepers Walk Carefully" and some of the other less dishevelled poems, to make very nice music indeed. Sometimes, however, he runs a good thing into the ground. In "Poetry Hotel," for instance, he begins with his best cadence and imagery —

I think there are webs in the sky like hotel rooms
where lemur eyes grow in the womb of nostalgia,

— but lets it degenerate into one metaphor after another till the reader forgets where he's been. Sometimes the poems are little more than notes for poems; and occasionally, when he loses the perspective that makes him such an original, Rosenblatt reeks of a dead serious I-am-a-lost-soul attitude. But on the whole it's wonderful stuff, one of his most textured collections to date.

The Globe and Mail, 1974

vi

Quite unwittingly, that authoritarian source, the style-book of *The Globe and Mail*, has something to say about two main varieties of modern poet. A celebrant, writes an anonymous news-room grammarian, is "one who presides over a religious rite. A celebrator is a maker of whoopee." Until now Susan Musgrave's most ambitious collection of poetry has been *Entrance of the Celebrant*, published last year, and she has been very much like the celebrant of her title: mysterious and brooding, concerned with dark rituals, private devotions and the cult of the imagination. Her poems came in several primary colours, but muted ones through which light streaked and was diffused. Superficially, her poems served the same purpose as stained-glass windows in mediaeval cathedrals: they drew the Philistines inside for more serious matters by the use of colour otherwise lacking in drab lives. In her new book, *Grave-Dirt and Selected Strawberries*, she continues to be all those things while moving into a transitional lyric stage and ending up, amazingly, a *de facto* celebrator.

The whoopee she manufactures in the third section of the new book is merriment, good times and pure chicanery. There is only the slightest touch of the surreal imagism one finds in, for one, Stanley Cooperman, whose fun is the result of frustration with politics and contemporary culture. Nor does the "Selected Strawberries" part of the book display the sly wit one finds frequently in a poet like Earle Birney. Hers is more like found and pop poetry, in which she substitutes the word "strawberry" for the key words in maxims, quotations and clichés, and parodies the *Guinness Book of Records*, one of the Oxford dictionaries and various other works of reference. There are also "real" poems on strawberry themes. It's light stuff, of course, but skilfully arranged; and it brings one speedily out of the psychic depths

Musgrave investigates in the first section of the book and tries to bridge with the second.

In the "Grave-Dirt" part of the book, as in *Entrance of the Celebrant* and somewhat more so than in her earlier *Songs of the Sea Witch* (1971), Musgrave is a meditative poet who makes the reader think hard, squint, relax and think some more about a poem in order to get inside it and appreciate it. Yet she does not let her language get out of hand. She writes not diary entries but actual poems, structured things that require just as much work on her part. She resists (though sometimes just barely) the temptation to write a book each time she writes a poem. That is, she resists the call of a contemporaneity that would have her drop stricter forms for loose sequences and poem cycles, that would have her writing poetry that only works in big groups of little pieces rather than individual poems that stand up by themselves. One example of the temptation withstood is the poem "Equinox," included here, which was published as a pamphlet in Britain two years ago. Another, better example is "Grave-Dirt" itself:

One god
distributes the light.
By error on that day
he descends into hell.

Hell is just an impression

luck-balls from the
death-owl's mask.

Raven unsheaths his
beak-knife,
his voice is made of
glass . . . .

Here, as in her poetry generally, she displays a peculiar talent for expressing an inner drama, a tension completely self-contained and born of nothing from outside except whatever it is that sets her mind to working up these moods. Usually this works well, as it does in the title poem, with its suggestion of tribal imagery. When the poem depends on the conveyance of that imagery alone, however, as in the fourteen "Kiskatinaw Songs" of the centre section, the effect is not nearly so impressive. This is a group of poems based on myths of the west coast Indians and including a creation legend, a fertility legend and so on. The same dramatic technique is here, but somehow it just doesn't work. This is probably because the Songs are just that. They are too close to an oral tradition that lacks, in print, density; and lacks, a cappella, the ability to make moods in the reader's mind. Song and poem are given too much credit for having something in common, but this is an easy mistake for a contemporary poet, envious of musicians, to make.

Susan Musgrave is only twenty-two and has been for some time held up as one of the most promising young Turks. It has even been suggested that she is the next major poet of English Canada. Certainly she has grown tremendously in a short time, changing her voice and digesting the large chunks she has bitten off, and she has created a medium-large body of work in relation to her age. But until *Grave-Dirt and Selected Strawberries*, Musgrave had published no book of noticeable versatility, nothing that was (regardless how it was intended) a collection instead of an accumulation. Now she has.

Saturday Night, 1974

vii

There's an elemental lesson about Al Purdy's poetry to be learned by paging through the files of certain literary magazines of the past twenty-five years or so. In the earliest days of his career, Purdy gave his name, in all its Loyalist splendour, as Alfred Wellington Purdy. But he quickly condensed this to Alfred W. Purdy. Then came a long period of uncertainty and experiment when, with equal ease, he answered in print to both Alfred W. and A.W. Purdy. It's only been in the 1970s that his byline has become completely stable in its least formal incarnation, just plain Al. Concurrent with what otherwise would seem this simple exercise in marketing, another and more important form of ecdysis was taking place as well. As Purdy was reducing his name to its simplest and most appropriate form, he was undertaking to do the same to his poetry, freeing himself of some badly chosen early influences and a lot of unnatural speech. To go back today and reread him, watching the reductive process by which he finds his distinctive style and rightful voice, is to experience a quiet, cumulative excitement.

The turning point in this process occurred in 1968. In that year he published two important books: *Wild Grape Wine*, at once his most cohesive and broadest-ranging collection, and *Poems for All the Annettes*. The latter, a revised and expanded version of an earlier book of the same title, brought together in final form, and in his new diction, all the poems he wished to preserve up to about 1965. It is therefore a companion volume to his new book, *Being Alive: Poems 1958-78*, even though there's some overlapping. The difference between them is that, despite a few revisions Purdy cannot resist making, the new book is not reworked, warmed-over Purdy the way the other was. It's more than a fitting testament to his work up to now, but it's not just a pause for reflection at age sixty. It shows him in his present stride as a craftsman and a poetic personality, continuing the struggle to reach some sort of agreement with history.

A concern with how to find roots in an uprooted past, and what to do with them, seems to have always been central to many Canadian poets, and not simply to the obvious ones. With Purdy the question is nothing short of a daily obsession. He certainly has every right to feel a special closeness to the eastern part of Ontario he's particularly associated with. His family, after all, has been there forever. There's even a hamlet called Purdy in the Country North of Belleville (though it's not mentioned in his famous poem of that title); it's near the farm once worked by his grandfather, the "ugly grandfather who was 250 pounds of scarred lumberjack/hell-raiser and backwoods farmer" and the subject of several poems.

But Purdy goes beyond this in his historical awareness. One of the differences between him and other poets is that, in his case, environment has combined with his marvellous self-acquired education to produce a feeling for folklore. This is apparent in the anthropological turn he takes in many of his poems on native peoples and early explorers and in the ones arising from travels overseas. It's obvious in another sense, too — in other poems — to the extent that he makes *himself* a character from folklore, a sort of updated, Canadian version of Chaplin's Little Tramp, and a most unrepresentative Everyman. This is the comic Purdy of such memorable poems as "At the Quinte Hotel," which is written from a standpoint of inebriation but which (or perhaps therefore) is always a favourite at readings.

I am drinking
I am drinking beer with yellow flowers
in underground sunlight
and you can see that I am a sensitive man
And I notice that the bartender is a sensitive man too

Such a tatterdemalion pose allows Purdy to comment on everyday misadventures and non-adventures. But even when writing about marital spats and the like, he's never very far from a serious purpose: married life, in Purdy's poems, is often an unconscious metaphor for the way history accumulates, the way things always go on but never remain the same. When he writes prose, which he does from time to time, Purdy tries using this same persona, but he's never so successful. His grammar looks dilapidated and the syntax always seems to have its shirt-tail hanging out. The problem is not that he lacks style; it's that he loses interest in writing what isn't poetry, what doesn't put his eye and his ear to working in unison.

To think of Purdy as a craftsman has never been very fashionable, but this just shows the folly of conventional wisdom. Many of his longer poems especially, such as "Hombre," his powerful obituary for Che Guevara, are marvellously put together, with jaggedness and mellifluousness played off against each other and repetition cleverly deployed. The result is the prose-like but hypnotic pace that's characteristic of his poems, a rhythm which, along with the particular use he makes of idiomatic language, could be called influential. This, too, is seldom said: that the effect of Purdy can easily be seen in poets as diverse as Andrew Suknaski and Dennis Lee. Perhaps the hesitation is due to the way Purdy operates to some extent outside the literary bullring with not only its high mortality rate but its spoils system. He goes his own way, lending a hand to others but asking little for himself, seeming not to care very much if he's called an establishment figure or a liberal softie. And he thrives in the ways he believes are important. If there's one conclusion to be drawn about Purdy from *Being Alive* it's that he's that rare creature in literary circles, a truly happy man, unmarked by rancour, living a well-considered life, trying to make sense of his past and his present.

Saturday Night, 1978

viii

There must be times when Irving Layton hears his career ululating above him as though it were his spirit and he were having an out-of-body experience. That's how wide the gap sometimes is between the private Layton one finds in his best poetry and the public Layton one finds almost everywhere else. That's how much the career has always seemed to have a separate life of its own. The latest reminder of this is *Taking Sides*, a collection of his fugitive letters, speeches and articles. It's a curious volume, full of apparent contradictions. It's stubborn and ornery, and it has little to do with poetry, but it does have one significant grace: it throws light not so much on the nature of the man himself as on the course of his career. It provides almost a shadow biography.

By covering a period of more than forty years, the book either clears up or reminds us of several facts about Layton's career. The most basic point is that his beginnings were pre-Can lit; his career began in another generation, when the media and the reputation-makers couldn't have cared less. Layton's response was simply to go about *acting* famous until he actually *became* famous. This method he pioneered is one several other Canadian writers have since followed. No one, though, has been more successful at baiting the media into patronizing him so that he can take umbrage and thus call still more attention to his serious work.

Layton's first political focus was Europe in the 1930s. He was a dedicated anti-Fascist, but even if he'd not been, such a stance would have been presumed: most people routinely believe that poets are naturally left wing. In later years, when he went on to make probably a more significant contribution to Canadian poetry than anyone else his generation, he still remained the very image of the Poet to people who never read the stuff. He remained so despite the fact that his politics quickly shifted to the right. By the late 1960s and 1970s one finds him offending everyone he's not already quarrelled with in the past. He strongly supports the Americans in Vietnam, praising Lyndon Johnson and wishing "perdition to all his enemies," even applauding the invasion of Cambodia. He claims to sympathize with the women's movement but only "when it's not dominated by freak-outs or just plain nasty graceless sluts." He also manages to endorse both the Parti Québécois and Trudeau's use of the War Measures Act.

Unlike many poets, Layton is an entertaining writer of prose, but that side of him was already displayed to its best advantage in *Engagements*, a collection of his stories, prefaces and essays, selected by Seymour Mayne and published in 1972. By contrast, *Taking Sides*, edited and introduced by Howard Aster, is pretty slapdash, and when not that, marginal in the extreme. A condensed version of Layton's 1946 MA thesis on Harold Laski, for instance, is the most substantial piece. The rest ranges from some casual talks to endless letters to the editor of the Montreal *Star*. But while it may be peripheral material it still makes various statements about the nature of his career.

One would expect, for instance, that someone so deliberately obstreperous as Layton — someone who's used his reputation to make an image and his image to build a career — would take the so-long-as-they-spell-my-name-right approach to personal publicity. Nothing could be further from the truth. Here one sees again his distressing habit of failing to take it as well as dish it out, as when he attacks reviewers who give him any less than full-blown praise. There are subtler points, too. In one place, for example, he informs his audience that his field is actually political science (in which he did postgrad work), that he came to poetry on the rebound. The message is that he wants to be taken seriously as a public figure, not just as a celebrity, and that being a public issue, even if one has to force the notion, is perhaps one way of achieving this. This is the subconscious theme of many of these pieces and the overall thrust of *Taking Sides*.

What we have here is a Citizen Layton, saying what he believes in, certainly, but also what he believes he should say in order to jar the audience from its complacency. This has proved a good technique in poetry, which is not taken very seriously by any sort of mass audience. It has not served him so well, though, in politics, which most Canadians hold more precious than breath itself. It's one thing for Layton to commit himself to the idea that "really good poetry disturbs people, shakes them up and breaks down certain habits and associations in their minds [and reminds them] that disgust, hatred, violence and even vice are permissible roads to salvation." It's quite another for him to believe the same style will work in politics, which by nature is concerned less with life than with — well, the opposite of life.

Yet one can sympathize with Layton, whose pronouncements become louder with time. His place is secure as a poet and as a friend to poetry. Long gone is the day he was widely held to be a trouble-making beatnik pinko of the arts. Like many other artists, though, he wishes to be both outrageous and respected at the same time but has found that the one usually precludes the other. Politics, then, serves the dual function of providing him with new means of debunking and emoting and of allowing him to seem more public, more serious, more *complete*, as a figure and as a reputation. The difference, of course, is that the politicking is not an end in itself. Even the relatively recent pieces in *Taking Sides* seem terribly dated and transient. None of them stands up alongside a good Layton poem or even a lesser one. Surely that is the lesson to be learned.

Saturday Night, 1978

ix

It seems Earle Birney has been writing his memoirs for a long time but releasing them in a piecemeal fashion. Throughout the 1970s, one would see him trudging off to the rare books room of the University of Toronto library to consult his accumulated papers, and occasionally one would catch a glimpse of something autobiographical in print (as in a curious little book titled *The Cow Jumped Over the Moon* or, more recently, in his prose collection *Big Bird in the Bush*). Now comes *Spreading Time: Remarks on Canadian Writing & Writers, Book One: 1904–1949*. Ostensibly it is a collection of old reviews, articles, columns and radio talks about Can lit of the period, and as such gives some interesting contemporary opinion on figures of the day. But the real value is the other 50 per cent of the book, made up of Birney's scene-setting reminiscences, for this can easily be taken as another small instalment of his memoirs.

As such, it is the story of the poet's early years and of his struggle not so much to be a distinctly Canadian writer as to find some distinctly Canadian writing to be a part of. At seventy-six Birney is old enough to have a past compounded of tiny associations that are themselves historically appealing. As a youngster, for instance, he sold copies of Bob Edwards's Calgary *Eye-Opener* on the street. He was born in Calgary, though his parents lived first on a farm and later, when Birney was seven, moved to Banff, then a village of about 500 people. There's a healthy outdoorsy feel to the whole story, which is becoming to the author of "David." There's also a great sense of frustration at being so remote from whatever literary life the country had to offer.

The household was a somewhat bookish one, though not pretentiously so. Birney easily picked out Lampman and D.C. Scott as being several cuts above the rest of the Maple Leaf School prevalent at the time, and he credits his English father with making him aware that "there was a novelist in the country who could write with realism about prairie farming (his name at that time was Grove), and another man in the farthest East with the unpoetic name of Pratt, who had nevertheless written a moving and original poem called 'Newfoundland.'"

Birney gets the bug when he attends the University of British Columbia and comes under the spell of one particularly worldly professor. But the itch is only made worse after scratching by some of the travelling poets of the day. Wilson MacDonald, Bliss Carman and Carman's cousin Charles G.D. Roberts all visit the coast, but they strike Birney as posturing buffoons out to wring coppers from an audience of yahoos. He feels only slightly less outside the world of letters after going east and meeting some of the other young writers of the period, such as Raymond Knister, Roy Daniells, Robert Finch and Dorothy Livesay. In time he becomes an editor of *The Canadian Forum* and finds a more solid, interdisciplinary sort of fellowship. It makes a fascinating little chapter in Canadian intellectual history.

Birney's life has been one of the most curious and full in Canadian poetry. But though the period covered in the book is 1904 to 1949, he glosses over the fact that he spent seven of those years in radical political circles, some of them as an organizer, an experience which produced his novel *Down the Long Table*. And he all but totally ignores the Second World War, out of which came *Turvey*. He makes hardly anything of his peculiar life as itinerant teacher and revolutionary (and one-time CBC worker); we get nothing of the Chaucerian scholar committed to the real world, none of the stories about Trotsky, Sherwood Anderson and Emma Goldman he's been telling privately for years. One reason is that he may now be somewhat embarrassed by some of his early affiliations. Perhaps a more important reason, though, is that Birney, one of the oldest practising Canadian poets, is likewise one of the youngest. Through the 1960s and 1970s he explored every new technique and took part in almost every new literary trend, keeping himself more agile and productive than most figures half his age. As a writer, he was a relatively late starter, then a slow plodder through the 1940s and 1950s, and has been a vital force ever since. For such a person, an autobiography must seem inconsistent with keeping a fix on the present, or possibly an invitation to bad luck. This is all quite understandable, even laudable in a way, but inevitably it makes the work of sorting out his past a patchwork and not quite satisfying affair.

Saturday Night, 1980

X

The poet Bruce Whiteman, who works as a librarian at McMaster University, published a short article in *The Globe and Mail* not long ago concerning his third role, that of bibliographer. He wrote in defence of the tradition of the authored bibliography, citing the primary function of such books as "the writer's memory and the critic's or student's guide" (he might have also said the collector's or dealer's bible). He was speaking of the sort of bibliography that in some quarters it now is fashionable to call a check-list, as though to illustrate how the form has been corrupted. A genuine bibliography, annotated and with as much detail as possible about editions, states and first appearances, is a thing of beauty in itself and often a revealing mirror of the person whose works are being scrutinized. This is certainly the case with Whiteman's own *Collected Poems of Raymond Souster: Bibliography* and Fraser Sutherland's *John Glassco: An Essay and a Bibliography*. Both have significant value as reference works but offer more than that. The Souster one can be read as a partial biography of its subject, the Glassco one as a revisionist criticism.

To use the Souster bibliography as a narrative one need only remember a few basic facts: that Souster was born in Toronto in 1921 and that he fell in with Canadian and foreign modernists not too long after joining one of the major banks where, except for time out during the Second World War, he has laboured since 1939. The pattern of his literary career is quite bankerly in that the power of his verse lies in the decades-long process of accumulation and the ledger-like neatness with which the poems are tallied in book form at regular intervals. But it pleases many to see the fact that he's a poet and a bank worker as somehow indicative of contrary strains. Anyway, in 1935 Souster began publishing verse in both the Toronto *Star* and the *Mail and Empire*, papers diametrically opposed in everything, it would seem, except their willingness to accept his work. He appeared more often in the *Star* than in the *Mail and Empire*. He also published in the *Globe*, where he signed himself Sappho, possibly because it sounded literary to the fourteen-year-old mind.

The sort of poetic career that could flourish perversely on a life in banking found no obstacle in the armed forces. Quite the contrary, to judge from a letter Whiteman quotes. Souster is in the RCAF, stationed in Nova Scotia, and writes to a friend, "Since I've been posted here at Sydney I've had plenty of time on my hands for writing — more even than I had in civilian life. I've started a novel and the poems come now and then — altogether it keeps me busy." Bibliographies often reveal how writers in one form crave renown in some other, and Souster wrote two novels about which Whiteman gives all the tantalizing details. The first, in 1950, was *The Winter of Time*, published under the name Raymond Holmes by a sleazy Toronto paperback house that also brought out pseudonymous work by Hugh Garner and Brian Moore. The second, in 1973, was a starkly realistic RCAF novel called *On Target*, this time by *John* Holmes. It was done by Martin Ahvenus, the Toronto bookseller, in a trade edition and a limited edition, the latter signed not as Holmes but as Souster. For Souster of course had long since gained some popular acceptance after twenty years as a fixture of the small presses.

His first book publication was *Unit of Five* (Ryerson Press, 1944), in which he shared space with Louis Dudek, Ronald Hambleton, P.K. Page and James Wreford. Whiteman quotes from Lorne Pierce's correspondence to show that the grouping was not necessarily inspired by poetic compatibility.

As an editor, Pierce had been receiving manuscripts from a new generation of poets and for some reason felt he couldn't publish them separately in the Ryerson Chapbook series. Further correspondence suggests that the book sold very poorly indeed. Also, it seems to have been reviewed in, of all places, the Toronto *Board of Trade Journal*. Various other small books and booklets followed. One of them was *New Poems* (1948), of which only one copy could be located.

It seems that in 1947 Souster started up a little business called the Enterprise Agency to distribute literary magazines and small press publications, including some he himself planned to mimeo. These were the "forerunner of the Contact Press mimeographed books of the 1950s," before that press graduated to properly printed books with Dudek's edition of *The Selected Poems of Raymond Souster*. The Enterprise Agency was run in connection with a news-letter called *Enterprise: A Monthly Review*, a more obscure one than either his later *Combustion* or *Contact*, and it seems not to have lasted long. Whiteman believes that the Enterprise publications were "intended more for friends and colleagues than for the public." Souster himself, in a letter to Irving Layton, sees such methods as "one way of getting your stuff around to the other half a hundred people or so who are interested." But he published some of his work in an edition of only twenty-five, feeling *that* number sufficient to satisfy the market. Through this bibliography emerges a clear picture of Souster coming home every day, retreating to some basement or back room, scratching away at his poems and then bucking the world's indifference as to whether or not the flame was kept alive. It is a timely picture.

A bibliography such as this is important for its confirmations of what's already known but also for its fresh titbits and new connections, since all such information together shows the pattern of a writing career. It's interesting to learn, for example, that in 1946 Souster should have appeared in a communist anthology entitled *Spirit of Canadian Democracy*. Or to see proof of the extent to which by the early 1950s he was in touch with, and in league with, the international poetry underground as typified by Robert Creeley and, especially, Cid Corman.

Throughout this period he would seem to have received mainly intramural or local notice. Some of his books were being reviewed in a journal called *The Deer and Dachshund*, and as late as 1962 one of his important collections, *Place of Meeting*, was published by the Isaacs Gallery in Toronto rather than by any remotely mainstream publisher. But all that changed when Ryerson brought out *The Colour of the Times* in 1964 and followed up with *Ten Elephants on Yonge Street* in 1965. Then he began getting reviews in newspapers outside Toronto and in *Maclean's* and *Saturday Night*. He began getting a non-professional audience, and the books were reprinted more than once. When its Protestant masters sold Ryerson Press, in what seemed the most cold-hearted assault on the arts since the dissolution of the monasteries, Souster was luckier than most. He had already found a steady publisher in Oberon Press, which has made a tremendous commitment to publishing his work, a commitment now rounded out with this fine bibliography, which is certainly no less than such a good and selfless man deserves.

The Glassco bibliography is of a different order and has a different lesson to teach. The first part of the book is a biographical sketch of Glassco, an appreciation of him as a stylist and an argument for higher rank. It is a credible job, written with great affection for the work and the person. Sutherland avoids controversy in dealing with someone who was a pornographer as well as a poet, albeit a pornographer of the *fin de siècle* literary kind. The bibliography comprising the second portion of the book, including an inventory of the Glassco papers at McGill and other repositories, cannot escape some implied controversy, though it is presented without comment.

Glassco's most famous work, of course, is *Memoirs of Montparnasse*, the on-the-spot autobiography he began writing in Paris in 1928. Fragments were published at the time but the work was not completed, Glassco claimed later, until 1932. The whole manuscript was not published until 1970. At that time, many suspected it was of more recent vintage than he suggested, as it was written in a fully mature style; Louis Dudek took the trouble to compare the originally published fragment with the same section in the completed book and found them almost wholly dissimilar. But that was only one chapter. Sutherland's work in the Glassco papers, however, does tend to show that Glassco was perhaps less than candid in not suggesting that *Memoirs* was, to a good extent, a work of the 1960s inspired by something older.

Of course, that detracts from the book not at all. But it does speak to the central critical notion that seeps up between the lines of this bibliography: the fact that part of Glassco's art was his playing with the text, his playing with the very *idea* of a text. There is some question whether what he maintained were his first two books, *Conan's Fig* (1928) and *Contes en crinoline* (1929), ever actually existed; no copies are known to have survived. But this is fitting for someone who practised pornography in a certain environment and at a certain period and mixed it with literature. It was subterfuge as much as style perhaps that links Glassco the writer of poems and translations to Glassco the writer of dirty books. Glassco might even have found that deception was the greater part of prurience.

It was typical of underground writing and publishing generally that he should have found it necessary to describe *Temple of Pederasty* as a translation from the Japanese when in fact it was his original work. But it was typical of him particularly, with what now seems his pronounced bump of impishness, that he should have published something called *Fetish Girl* under the pseudonym Sylvia Bayer while dedicating it to one John Glassco. It does not seem that he shared any impulse with Frederick Philip Grove in such matters, and to do further detective work is probably to miss the point. The point is only that the poet and pornographer was also sort of — what could the term be? — a self-inflicted forger. Readers knew this was an obvious piece of his equipment as a stylist; that's what made it possible for him to finish Beardsley's unfinished *Under the Hill*. But it was also, we know now thanks to this bibliography, a more important part of his outlook and his art.

Fraser Sutherland synopsises reviews of some of Glassco's books. Of the poems in *A Point of Sky*, he quotes a 1966 review by bill bissett in which bissett states, "They all look like bad trips to me," advising Glassco to "get the air thru yr windew no english literature its du you/feel good." Certainly Glassco seems just as well anchored to "english literature" as ever (that is his strength, surely). But he now also appears to have been more of an antiquary and, in his almost post-modern relationship to text, more of an experimenter too.

Books in Canada, 1984

SIX

Notes on Dennis Lee

i

The poet-publisher — not the self-publicist but the poet who, as it happens, runs a bona fide publishing firm — is very much a contemporary figure about whom, beyond this simple statement, it is dangerous to generalize. Some examples (Louis Dudek in Montreal) are better known as writers than as publishers of books, though in their latter roles they have carried on tirelessly for years. Others, in Canada and elsewhere, are more widely known as business- than as literary men. Somewhere between the two extremes is Dennis Lee, the Toronto publisher with a reputation for ferreting out, sweating over and presenting in book form the works of some of the country's best young writers, anglophone and francophone alike.

So significant is much of his own poetry and so valuable much of his publishing that it is difficult to say in which field he has done the better work. Equally difficult is determining if his activities with House of Anansi Press have infringed upon his writing (two statements in his new book, *Civil Elegies and Other Poems*, could be interpreted this way). What is more certain is that until now his poet's reputation has suffered at the hand of his editor's one, that he has been too seldom published, too little recognized and too little read. The main impact, I think, of this new collection will be to swing opinion the other way and, perhaps, even the score.

Half the book is made up of the Civil Elegies, nine long ruminations on and inquiries into modern Canadian life, much influenced by the thinking of George Grant and others. Undoubtedly Lee's major work, they are haunting, anguished and (appropriately) elegiac poems written in loping, sweeping lines and in which semantics, I believe, are important. For instance, the word "civil" in the title could have many meanings, yet is not a play on words so much as a one-word definition of the complete impetus behind the poems themselves. They are civil in the sense that they are about the city, and the narrator used the civic square of Toronto's city hall as a departure and landing point; and civil in the sense that Lee is a civilian speaking to other civilians, worn out and worried by personal and party politics and the natural attrition of life, matters over which he may not have even the most infinitesimal control. Lee, like the rest of us, has no answers, but he states the problems with eloquence.

Three of the elegies are new and are published here for the first time; the others have been greatly fiddled with and generally improved since their appearance in a 300-copy edition in 1968, the year after *Kingdom of Absence* (the author's and Anansi's first book) came out in a similarly small edition. It is interesting that "Sibelius Park," one of the most complex of the sixteen "private poems" that comprise the first half of the present volume, was first issued as a broadsheet, that Lee here too used the hallowed limited edition as Broadway uses New Haven.

These "other" poems of the title are dedicated *Illisque pro annis uxore* ("For my wife and those years") and are mainly love-desperation poems in which Lee's technical mastery is at its best and most obvious. He is nearly unique among Canadian poets of consequence in knowing when to use to best effect either the disjointed, abrupt modern lyric or its opposite, the long descriptive or narrative line. The latter he employs, as he does in the elegies, for long continuous statements that make their own moods as they go along; the former he uses superbly for his own brand of surrealism, one born of trying to cope with contemporary civilization on a day to day basis. In these poems he gets across his frustration by somehow lapsing into the ludicrous during the normal course of a poem or by repeatedly slipping away in mid-sentence as new thoughts attack him *en masse* from all sides like schools of piranha.

But to me the most important property of these poems, both the elegies and the single poems, is Dennis Lee's voice. Although his language is both colloquial and intellectual, he neither talks down to the reader nor confronts him with formality. Rather, it is as if the reader has just happened into the room where the poet's mind is discoursing on its own state, for its own good, with great common sense and no real self-pity. In all the poems, the elegies concerned with big problems common to us all and in the little poems taken up with domestic matters, the voice is the same. It is like no one else's.

Saturday Night, 1972

ii

No other literary career in memory has been quite like the one Dennis Lee has had during the past decade. Scarcely anyone has been more influential intellectually. No one has launched so many new writers or anonymously shaped so many other people's manuscripts or so singlehandedly set the tone of serious publishing. Although he is known to the broad public as a composer of verse for children, it is difficult to think of another poet with the high sense of purpose and craft that Lee shows in his more serious collections. One is similarly hard pressed to find anyone else whose views are a better indication of the social and political thought common among younger Canadian writers.

Lee is unique even while he's a part of (and symbol for) a great many currents in our artistic life. Yet for all that, the ideas traceable throughout his work have never been made available to the general reader in a simple, easily digestible manner. His first critical work, *Savage Fields: An Essay in Literature and Cosmology*, though in many ways a dense book, goes a long way towards showing what makes Dennis Lee tick, especially when put in the context of his earlier writings.

He was part of the University of Toronto mafia. Emerging into the real world in the early 1960s, he found it a far less likeable place than he had remembered from his stable and protected childhood. He was part of the group that, in order to sort out their confusion, escaped briefly to Britain or the United States. Lee chose England, and while there he wrote what later became his first book of poetry, *Kingdom of Absence* (1967), which explored the sense of being lost in the crack between his background and his environment. It appeared at a time when, like many of his contemporaries, he was caught up, cautiously at times but not half-heartedly, in various sorts of radical political action. He co-founded, for instance, both the House of Anansi Press, which changed the shape of Canadian publishing, and Rochdale College, which for a time appeared to be a new direction in education. Slowly, though, he came to reject, as did many other writers, what began to seem this artificial and alien tradition. Unlike, say, those 1930s radicals who found no immediate substitute for their topical beliefs and gave up the search, Lee continued to question the meaning of his dilemma. He came to see himself eventually as more or less a red tory — a red tory being one who, by voting NDP because it is the party of his intellectual station, is free to be a tory without fear of being tarred a Progressive Conservative. His mentors and contemporaries in related fields in time made peace with the problem. As a philosopher, George Grant found redress and comfort in Christianity. As a fiction writer, Margaret Atwood found hers in a particular strain of feminism. As a journalist, Charles Taylor discovered his in a reworking of certain British traditions.

But Lee has never come out with a finite solution. His continued search is the spark in many of his writings and gives them their special urgency and sense of humanity. In *Civil Elegies* (1968, revised 1972) he said no to liberalism and eloquently confessed to a feeling of emptiness over the question of how to live a good and useful life in a society whose direction he does not like. Later, in *The Death of Harold Ladoo*, published in 1976, he spoke from the same private source on more public matters that plagued him. This long poem was in a way the bridge between *Absence* and the *Elegies* on the one side and, on the other, *Savage Fields*, which is a further rejection of modernity and an attempt to place his intellectual discomfort in a more universal context. Whereas the *Elegies* concerned Lee's difficulties in trying to find himself as a Canadian human being, the new book deals with the same question as regards a human being who happens to be Canadian.

Ostensibly, *Savage Fields* is a critical study of Michael Ondaatje's *The Collected Works of Billy the Kid* and Leonard Cohen's *Beautiful Losers*. On the surface their appropriateness to Lee's ideas is that the first finds order in a recent mythic past and the other in crazy sexuality. But the argument is much more complex than this, just as the book is more than a scholarly exercise. The savage fields of the title are the no-man's land between "world" (that is, civilization, reason, life and order) and "earth" (nature, instinct, death and perpetual chaos). Simply put, Lee sees the tussle between the two psychic poles as the central characteristic of modern existence. In fact, he believes it so ingrained that experimental and "prophetic" writers such as Cohen and Ondaatje write of and from it without being aware of doing so. "*Billy the Kid* does not explain why the savage fields exist; it doesn't even ask why in any serious way. It simply assumes, with a magisterial finality which seems beyond special pleading, that this is what our planet is like now. The only task it sets itself is to create images of that planet in action." Lee does not, given that, bend these books to suit his argument. He presumes what he believes Ondaatje and Cohen accept subconsciously. Perhaps partly as a result, his chapters on the books are critical jewels, offering genuinely new insights and fresh textual interpretations. It is especially rewarding to read so lovingly conceived a critique of *Beautiful Losers*, which was met in Canada with almost unanimous hostility when it first appeared and has been subjected to various abuses since then.

As the subtitle indicates, however, *Savage Fields* is an essay in cosmology as well as literature, and the two books are merely touchstones for Lee's ideas on the insidiousness of technology, the unobtainable nature of personal peace and the mercurial quality of history as applied to our present condition. Although it may go no further than his poetry in making solutions from these ideas, it is more ambitious in trying to pin-point the exact texture of being, as Lee sees it. Using two popular works of art to do so seems a natural enough technique for a literary man hunting territory in common with his readers. There are, however, serious problems in the structure.

Many of the concepts in *Savage Fields* stem from the works of those philosophers, especially Grant and Heidegger, who have influenced him. But Lee claims that the framework was suggested by reading Ondaatje and Cohen, that he did not first make the mould and then find examples to fit it. He began the book in 1972 with the intention of also discussing the works of Graeme Gibson, Chris Scott, Russell Marois and Lawrence Garber, among others. Then he limited himself to dealing with only six books and finally with just the two. Partly as a result, *Savage Fields* is compact and indeed almost impacted; one has a sense of its having been condensed but never fully reconstituted. Lee struggles nobly to make himself clear and create a voice true to his thoughts, with varying results.

Often he recaptures unflinchingly the personal intensity characteristic of his poetry. At other times he manages to achieve only a blend of familiarity and abstract ideas that is a little jarring and occasionally funny. This, for example, is a note from the back of the book on *Beautiful Losers*: "In superficial terms, he lifts Catherine/Isis's veil in Book Three when he goes down on the blonde in the Oldsmobile." But one cannot help thinking that the examples are too few and the canvas too small to show everything the author wishes to communicate.

Savage Fields is most rewarding for the incredible range of isolated ideas and the one big idea that permeates Dennis Lee's career. What Big Idea? In its simplest, least political form, nothing new. In the thirteenth century, Emperor Frederick II of the Holy Roman Empire conducted an experiment to determine whether Hebrew was the natural language of man. He placed six new-born infants in isolation for years, allowing them no human contact except with one another and with foster mothers who were forbidden to speak in their presence. When finally the door was opened, the children, of course, were mad. A certain strain of experimental novelist (and, one sometimes get the feeling, Lee) would have thought the emperor successful at least in proving that surreal insanity is the true tongue of mankind. The only question is whether, in a certain cultural sense, he might not have been correct.

Saturday Night, 1978

iii

Dennis Lee is one of the country's most respected and influential poets. He is also one of Canada's most popular writers, though not necessarily for the same books. A wide range of his literary fellows practically worship him as a poet with a particularly contemporary, and especially tortured, form of political and religious sensibility (he is essentially that rare creature, a confessional and religious poet). They also acknowledge his key role as an editor and critic, one who has exerted a considerable influence on other people's work. This is the Lee who, two years ago when he was only forty-three, became the subject of a *Festschrift* to which colleagues such as Margaret Atwood and Irving Layton contributed glowing essays. This Lee receives such a voluminous correspondence on serious literary matters that he is threatening to employ a secretary.

But there is another Dennis Lee who is beloved on a different plane and by a very different audience, as the author of memorable collections of children's verse, *Wiggle to the Laundromat, Alligator Pie, Nicholas Knock and Other People, Garbage Delight* and, most recently, *Jelly Belly*. These books have sold hundreds of thousands of copies, generated a successful theatrical venture and lately have given Lee an entirely new career as a writer for television and film. This Lee is Canada's best-known writer among nine-year-olds, an astounding number of whom write to ask his advice, or thank him or to send him verses of their own.

The give and take between the two Lees, or between the two audiences and two kinds of renown, might easily lead to an identity crisis in another writer, but not Lee. "I enjoy doing both folk art — most kids' poetry is folk art — and high art." He sighs a bit. "I'd love it if I could do a little in each area all the time, but I can't." Not that he hasn't tried. The whole pattern of his career has been to undertake more than one thing at a time. Such work habits are somehow bound up with the moral unease he feels and his powerful yearning to communicate it.

Lee is a gently rounded pipe smoker with a beard and thinning flaxen hair, and he radiates a sharply intellectual kind of friendly cordiality. He was born in Toronto in 1939. Both grandfathers and assorted other ancestors were Methodist preachers, and he himself "grew up in the suburban United Church and what ritual there was was of the most dessicated sort." To someone who has known him for a number of years, Lee has always appeared torn between his meditative side and his liturgical side. He has seemed like, so to speak, a High Church Methodist. One side of him is definitely a Dennis with two n's (middle class, Protestant, suburban and contemporary). The other is more of a Denis (patrician, Anglican, urban and antiquarian in taste). It is tempting to carry on with the comparison and say that one produces the imaginative rhymes for children, the other the intricate writing for serious adults; but that is simplistic, for there are elements of both in each sphere. The perceived difference, though, is real enough, as if it were the difference between what Lee was born and what he longs to become.

University of Toronto *Graduate*, 1984

SEVEN

The Vernacular Alden Nowlan

i

It seems impossible when listening to *Alden Nowlan's Maritimes*, the CBC's most recent record album of Canadian poetry, to remember that the New Brunswick poet is only thirty-nine years old. Not only does his voice sound like that of a man about sixty, it is the craggy, timeless voice of imagined metaphysics, a quicker, muddled version of the voice of the ghost in pursuit of someone to put his soul at rest, the off-camera voice from the grave in a Hammer film. All this, one would assume, is in distinct contrast with the type of poetry he writes, but no. There is a quality about his reading that brings to the twenty-four poems on this recording an element missed when one encounters them in print. The poems, nearly all of them, are about people and places in New Brunswick and his native Nova Scotia, generally the aged, sick or otherwise pathetic people and the rotting little places to which history has given only scars and oppressions, not security and pride. Nowlan's voice gets all this across without apparent effort. One must conclude that this is a natural result of the poet's affinity with the material and its sources, for as a performer Nowlan is not obviously gifted.

No actor could be found today to read the way he does. He has a fascinating accent that comes to the fore in the pronunciation of such words as "poem." He doesn't say "pome" or something close to "pome," as most of us would do, nor does he say "po-em," as a purist might; the word comes out closer to "po-awm," uttered with a sibilant slur and the mumble which, on first listen, makes a copy of the corresponding text useful. He does not declaim the poems at all but speaks them as he would speak over the telephone. Indeed, during the early poems on side A it may be difficult given a normal level of concentration to distinguish between the poems and the comments preceding them, a problem that the CBC could have avoided by allowing more time between cuts. Once or twice during "In Memoriam: Claude Orser (1894–1968)," an elegy for an ignorant, kindly backwater tinker, Nowlan's voice seems to falter, just slightly, with emotion.

The selections are well chosen, and cover probably the full range of his poetry and a wide span of years. Among them are "The Last Leper in Canada" and "The Mysterious Naked Man" (the title poem of one of his Clarke Irwin collections), both of which have an implied mystical flavour and show perhaps the direction in which his talent now travels. The final poem is "Ypres: 1915," which Nowlan recently chose as his own favourite. It is a half–tribute to the Canadians who held fast during the first German gas attack while all about them fled, and it is just far enough from corniness to be quite moving. Nowlan's rendering of it, or parts of his rendering of it, confirms an old suspicion that his line breaks and spacing have little to do with the way he actually expects the poems to be read but are simply what seem appropriate to the moment and the medium. The First World War poem is followed by Bruce Armstrong's reading of "The Gunfighter," from Nowlan's short-story collection *Miracle at Indian River* (1968); it is not one of his most memorable pieces of fiction. *Alden Nowlan's Maritimes* has liner notes by Robert Weaver.

Books in Canada, 1972

ii

The tributes to Alden Nowlan following his premature death last June all made mention of his position as a regional force in New Brunswick and the Atlantic provinces generally. But those that mentioned the other fact that so informed his work — the fact that he was, for many years, a working newspaperman — stopped just short of seeing its importance. At least to one who knew him only through his writing, he always appeared a latter-day representation of the strain of writer, less common now than fifty years ago, to whom the newsroom was the poor man's university. Moreover, this always seemed one of his strengths and part of his appeal. He was connected to a tradition, and he knew what to do with it. Such are the thoughts that come in reading the posthumously published *Early Poems*, edited by Robert Gibbs.

Gibbs makes clear in his preface that the original intention was merely to draw from a few of Nowlan's early books, published when he was still the editor of the weekly *Observer* in Hartland, New Brunswick. With Nowlan's death, however, the project took on more importance, and was extended to include selections from all six of his collections prior to *Bread, Wine and Salt*, the first of his Clarke Irwin titles, for which he received the Governor General's Award in 1968. With *Early Poems* it's certainly easy to see just how much of a pleasant shock *Bread, Wine and Salt* was, and what an advance over previous work, though it was the logical next step in a gradual process. *Early Poems* is a record of growth and as such is a positive document.

Nowlan's first book, published when he was twenty-five, was *The Rose and the Puritan* (1958), number four in the Fiddlehead chap-book series — which is somewhat like the fourth McDonald's hamburger ever sold. The selections from it show Nowlan to have been even then a well-modulated but sometimes passive champion of a certain Atlantic sensibility, though later he could also criticize the people he lived among and loved. Reading the poems from this period, I remembered a sentence from Nowlan's essay on the New Brunswick press in Walter Stewart's 1980 anthology, *Canadian*

Newspapers: The Inside Story. The line refers to a certain acquaintance of his as being "a Canadian man of letters in the old tradition: he had contributed short stories to *Blackwood's Magazine* and could build a birchbark canoe." Circumstances once encouraged such an approach. I wager that is the sort of writer the young Nowlan privately aspired to become. Yet the same tradition shielded him from what was happening outside.

He wrote boring ABAB quatrains and such, some of which remind one of Chesterton, others of which are full of a sort of orderly fire. (I wonder if he was reading Kenneth Leslie at the time?) The language is precise even when it's twisted to fit the form, though the contortions gradually disappear or become less visible. By his second book, *A Darkness in the Earth* (1959), he is writing in many different forms — even hymns — trying to find what suits him best, and the language manages to hit the mark several times, particularly when Nowlan is ironical. An example is "In the Hainesville Cemetery," wherein a Mrs Talbot comes to put flowers on what will one day be her own grave: "The Talbots are people/who make the beds before breakfast/and set the breakfast table/every night before they go to bed." The poems are becoming very — in a word — journalistic.

By *Wind in a Rocky Country* (1960) there are still some poems in rhyme, but these are giving way to little descriptive lyrics in purely contemporary language and also, most especially, to miniature poetic biographies. There are still occasional echoes of the High Style. For instance, a poem for his grandparents begins with the remark, "Their love was sister to the starving deer/and brother to December." The rhythm is more important than the sentiment or the sense. There is even some of this in *Under the Ice* (1961). ". . . I was born like sound/stroked from the fiddle to become the ward/of tunes played on the bear-trap and the hound" is one of several places where the words that make one think for a second run afoul of the cadence that makes one feel; finally one has to sit back and resign oneself to this process. *Under the Ice* is also the book in which New Testament imagery seems to enter the picture as a description of something within the writer himself, rather than as a concern of his neighbours that he is simply describing objectively. But the more noticeable feature of both *Under the Ice* and *The Things Which Are* the following year is the inclusion of more and more poetic biographical sketches and the rise of a more journalistic tone of voice, often in poems with ironic endings that cry out "ending," as in a feature story. From this point onward, the struggle is to use this more detached diction not in writing about others but in writing out of himself; the progress is slow but steady.

As most of the obituaries mentioned, Nowlan took a lot of pleasure in observing blue-collar New Brunswick people and remembering the Nova Scotians of his childhood. He saw wonderful diversity in not-quite-rural, not-quite-urban folks on the rim of official poverty. The same affection and understanding he felt towards them comes through in R.E. Blach's black-

and-white photos, taken during the 1930s and 1940s to judge by the look of them, that appear throughout *Early Poems*. As one goes through these poems and images, one sees Nowlan moving towards the derelicts of urban life. My suspicion is that this is preparing Nowlan for his years on the Saint John *Telegraph-Journal*, 1963 to 1968, where he seeks the newspaperman's aesthetic, which sees a stylized reality in the idea of the city as the haunt of lost souls, broken spirits and "characters" in general. This view begins to crop up in his poems in the 1960s, and later found expression in some of the stories in *Miracle at Indian River* (1968).

In a way, this is writing out of himself in that it is a stage he passed through between writing about his cousins, then about his parents, then about the purely external world — and then finding the interior one. By the time of *The Things Which Are* and his section of *Five New Brunswick Poets* (also 1962), Nowlan had actually arrived at the cumulative goal without losing anything he had earlier, except the technical mannerisms and forced diction, which needed losing. The poems from *The Things Which Are* and *Five New Brunswick Poets* — his last juvenilia, so to say — are more allegorical and more sequential; there is some standardization both in voice (a voice near that of the later Clarke Irwin books) and in technique (the poems all present much the same appearance on the page). From that point forward, Nowlan drew more widely for his material, sometimes going back into history. He also wrote more sure-footedly, with greater confidence, to the point where he could surprise us with the structure of his novel *Various Persons Named Kevin O'Brien* (1973) and have fun in the plays he wrote with Walter Learning.

In the process, he became the sort of all-rounder compatible with the nineteenth-century newspaper editor's image of himself, though by that time Nowlan was firmly settled into his long tenure as writer-in-residence at the University of New Brunswick.

There is a roundness and a wholeness about what he wrote that can be ascribed partly, I believe, to this inky persona in the back room of his imagination. His other posthumous book, for instance, is *Nine Micmac Legends*, illustrated by Shirley Bear. He retold the Indian myths in much the way Goldwin Smith translated Catullus: it was something to do when he had a minute. The act is squarely within the spirited layman's interest in such antiquarian pursuits as archaeology and anthropology, which in old English-Canadian newspapermen is roughly analogous to that of parish priests in Quebec. It is an attractive pose, and one that adds to the picture of Nowlan, who was neither the unworldly writer he was sometimes made out to be nor the rustic philosopher, but something much better and more serious. If the present books are not the full story, they certainly help to complete one's impression of an honest writer who found his footing and did his duty.

Books in Canada, 1984

EIGHT

Film Chronicle

i

"You in Canada should not be dependent either on the United States or on Great Britain," D.W. Griffith told a Toronto reporter in 1925. "You should have your own films and exchange them with those of other countries. You can make them just as well in Toronto as in New York City." Here the maker of *Intolerance* and *The Birth of a Nation* was being further ahead of his time than usual: until the Canadian film industry got under way, however haltingly and with all its well-known failures, images of the country derived mainly from foreign films in which Canada and Canadians somehow figured. Like the Hollywood Indian, the Hollywood Canadian was a sometimes comic, sometimes tragic figure who for those with any knowledge of the subject at all was so far removed from fact as to be both funny and sad in quite another way.

In knowing and caring less about its nearest neighbour than about its most distant, Hollywood was once again American society in crystallized form. Whenever a Canadian was called for in a film, Hollywood usually depicted him as a sort of substandard Englishman, a stereotype that was continued well into the 1960s (I recall in particular a cheap spy comedy of the period with an inefficient member of something called the Canadian Secret Service who was every bit as English as the Canadian chess master in the first James Bond film, *Dr No*). Yet sometimes Hollywood was inclined in quite the opposite direction as well. Bogart, certainly the least British of actors, played Canadians on three occasions, notably in *The African Queen*, and did so without any concessions to the character's nationality. Clearly the screen Canadian could be anything demanded by expediency, except believable as a native of Canada. British films were sometimes little better. Who can forget Robert Donat in Hitchcock's *The 39 Steps* when, as a Canadian, he mispronounces Winnipeg? Certainly not the shade of John Buchan, who as Lord Tweedsmuir became governor general the year this film was made from his novel.

The heyday of the screen Canadian would seem to have come in 1940, before the United States entered the Second World War. British propaganda films could use American actors in the role of allies or, as in Noel Coward's *In Which We Serve*, deal with a character who is American but feigns Canadianness in order to join the struggle against the Nazis. One is reminded of Bogart once again. In *Across the Pacific* (1942) he is a discredited American soldier who tries enlisting across the border only to be rejected by Hollywood's stereotypical Canadians. This is also the motion picture in which Bogart, rather cryptically, lisps to Mary Astor (who is posing as a native of Saskatoon), "There's a Canadian for you. You let them take off their clothes and they're happy." One is further reminded of Tony Curtis in the 1960 film *The Great Imposter*, the story of Ferdinand Demara, who posed as, among other things, a Royal Canadian Navy doctor; the real "Canadians" aboard are crisply British. The Canadian forces — foreign enough to be quaint, not so foreign as to be treacherous — have long held some attraction for American film-makers and presumably their audiences. But here again, the Canadians, as though citizens of Atlantis, are usually depicted as almost but not quite British, though it is an image that would appear to be fading. Compare the Canadian pilots in *Wings* (1927) with those in *Von Richtofen and Brown*, made two years ago. Of course, some of the change may be due to official indifference, compared to the Second World War period when the use of Canadians was a diplomatic concern of film-makers working for the British and Americans. Anything more may be just a lingering trace of what was once policy, or an instance of writing a Canadian into a script to justify the use of an American star where none would be called for otherwise. An example is *Attack on the Iron Coast* (1968), in which Lloyd Bridges of all people plays a Canadian commando leader unrecognizable as Canadian save by the flashes on his shoulders.

No doubt the richest mine of comparative film stereotyping in this sphere is *The Devil's Brigade* (1968), starring William Holden. It purports to deal with the fact that during the Second World War there was a joint Canadian-American force created for the purpose of invading Norway (they invaded Italy instead). The film is essentially no more than another American shoot-'em-up except that it is also, in its way, a statement on Canadian-American relations, albeit almost unintentionally so. Holden is a tough but gentlemanly American officer in overall command of a group of well-disciplined, ostentatiously uniformed Canadians and an equal number of undisciplined American ruffians. He is expected to whip the two components into a single unit. The Americans are played by such people as Claude Aikens and are an ungrammatical, slovenly lot who see the war as a lark, though one in which they take part unwillingly (fair enough you say). For their part, the Canadians include a Sgt.-Maj. Peacock with waxed mustachios; his charges include bonny highlanders who act and speak the way some American director would imagine Canadians to act and speak if he had considered it. Cliff Robertson appears as a Nova Scotian whose accent would baffle many a Nova Scotian. For comic relief and brotherhood, there is a tiny *québécois* who curses the Yanks in suspect French and who is protected from American harassment by his fellow countrymen.

Even more than Canadian soldiers, sailors and airmen, it is the Mounties of course who have held an attraction for Hollywood. *Rose Marie*, W.S. Van

Dyke's 1936 film in which Nelson Eddy warbles through the firs to Jeanette MacDonald (and which because of the popularity of one of the songs was re-released as *Indian Love Call*), is merely the best-known of a bad lot; it, or rather Friml's operetta on which it is based, was remade in 1954 by MGM, with Ann Blyth as the darling whose brother is lost in the North and Bert Lahr (Bert Lahr?) as the Mountie. More firmly rooted in actual history is *The Canadians* (1961), in which Robert Ryan and his fellows in scarlet keep in check the Sioux who have jumped the border after wiping out Custer. Then there was *Saskatchewan* (1954), in which Alan Ladd puts down the 1885 rebellion. Others within the reach of memory are *Mrs Mike*, about the lonely life of a Mountie's wife, and *Canadian Mounties vs Atomic Invaders*, perhaps the most awful Republic picture ever made and actually a serial re-edited from a previous product entitled *Missile Base at Tanlak*. As for Canadian history in general, Hollywood has misunderstood it as much as it has misunderstood its own, if not so often. Mindless as it is, *Quebec* (1951), concerning the troubles of 1837–38, could probably provoke an incident today, and Pierre Berton did well to mention as briefly as possible the existence of *Canadian Pacific* (1949) with Randolph Scott.

No, the only way Hollywood ever got even the slightest feel of Canada was accidentally, when dealing with topical situations. For instance, in *The Iron Curtain*, afterwards called *Behind the Iron Curtain*, a 1949 dramatization of the Igor Gouzenko affair starring Dana Andrews and Gene Tierney, the feeling of civil service Ottawa was so well duplicated that some scenes look as though they were filmed in Moscow. This is quite a different matter from simply inserting some footage of the Château Laurier, as in *Captains of the Clouds*, a 1941 film with Jimmy Cagney and with a cameo appearance by the real Billy Bishop. Most Hollywood films set in Canada, however, would seem to fail in their scenic credibility. I am thinking of earlier films such as the ludicrous Basil Rathbone–Nigel Bruce film *Sherlock Holmes and the Scarlet Claw*, nominally set in Quebec. Charles Boyer and Linda Darnell in *The 13th Letter* might as easily have been in a small American town as a small Quebec one given the accuracy of feeling. Nor did Robert Montgomery's Labrador weather station ring true in *Petticoat Fever* (1936), though this perhaps had more to do with the cheapness of the production values than with the quality of the thinking that went into the choice of geography.

All these films are of a kind apparently no longer made, though this does not mean that Hollywood has become any less ethnocentric, not if we are to judge by the fact that Margaret Laurence's novel *A Jest of God* was filmed in the States as *Rachel, Rachel*, with the setting changed, unaccountably and stupidly, from Manitoba to Maine. What is happening, rather, is that Canada itself is getting more parts than ever before. In the past the selection of Canada as a place to shoot a film carried with it a suggestion of the extraordinary. Houdini once made a daredevil movie of himself at Niagara Falls; Boris Karloff once appeared in a horror film shot at Casa Loma in

Toronto; and so on. Now many foreign feature films are being made in Toronto, Vancouver, Montreal, even Edmonton, due to certain financial and political machinery designed to attract them, due also to the ready availability of scenery and technical personnel at what seem cheap prices. One recent and typically lack-lustre example is the Paul Williams film *Dealing*, in which Toronto plays the role of Cambridge, Massachusetts, and the University of Toronto, Harvard. Seeing it, one must belatedly agree with what a commentator in the *Village Voice* observed years ago: that Toronto is not, as it secretly believes, a failed New York; it's a failed Boston.

Saturday Night, 1972

ii

Unable to fall asleep, I had finished with a current issue of *Harper's* dealing with the fall of Saigon and had turned to the late movie to find Peter Lorre as Mr Moto. It was part of that 1930s series about the obsequious Japanese detective, made to compete with the more successful series about Charlie Chan. The film was set in what is now Vietnam, a place depicted as a combination of India and Africa. The "natives" carried spears and round African shields made of hide, and their leader wore silks and a turban with a ruby on it. Then it came: a piece of dialogue that made me sit up in bed, laughing. There were two American newsmen, and one said to the other, "Let's take the canoes down to Saigon." *Canoes? To Saigon?* I fell asleep astounded that a mere forty years ago the United States could have made a film so totally ignorant of the place that would later so alter America's national life. Actually, I needn't have wondered, for the fact is that from the earliest days American films have treated Canada much the same way. The facts of this situation form the basis of *Hollywood's Canada*, by Pierre Berton, a book that sets out to explore the almost totally wrong-headed screen mythology of Canada.

Berton at once disregards those films set in other parts of the world in which Canadian characters appear. He undertakes to deal only with American-produced movies from early silent days to about 1960, and he examines these with considerable thoroughness. *Hollywood's Canada* comes up to the standards of detail we've come to expect from him. It is a masterpiece of time-consuming and expensive research, and it's unlikely that any other study will eclipse this in presentation of the great Hollywood-stereotype Canadians: the Mountie, the pseudo-Englishman and the half-mad French-Canadian trapper.

The longevity of these shallow characterizations, and the triumph of Hollywood's image of Canada over the reality, is easily shown by statistics alone. In his researches, Berton discovered 575 films set in Canada, beginning with a 1907 one-reeler called *An Acadian Elopement*. Ninety per cent of these films were set either in frontier towns or in the amorphous great outdoors. Seventy-five per cent were either filmed in the Rockies or conjured up the Rockies through the cheap magic of the backlot and the process shot. Of the 575 films (and Berton read synopses for most of those lost or destroyed), 256 involved Mounties in one way or another. These range from *North West Mounted Police* (1940), Cecil B. DeMille's first technicolour extravaganza, to my own personal favourite, *Canadian Mounties vs Atomic Invaders* (1953), another two A.M. television perennial and one perhaps only slightly more ludicrous than *Gene Autry and the Mounties* (1951). That most of these movies are dreadful is, of course, beyond question. They were nearly always B pictures, and many were cheapies even by the standards of the lesser studios such as Republic and Monogram. As Berton complains, they combined to give a glimpse of Canada as being, above all else, primitive. Railing against such dogged misrepresentation is what his book is about.

As his previous books have shown, Berton writes best when he writes of people. Fortunately, this story affords him three notable characters. The first is James Oliver Curwood (1878–1927), a Michigan pulp writer who inundated the fledgling motion picture companies with stories and scripts about a vaguely defined northland. Berton credits him with coining the phrase "God's Country," a claim I somehow doubt but cannot disprove. Curwood did more than anyone else to foster the image of a snowy dominion where tempers ran short and Mounties dashed about madly. It was a conception that outlived its popularizer by many decades. It was one to which the second figure stood in violent opposition.

This was Bruce Carruthers, a former RCMP officer who established himself in Hollywood as a free-lance technical adviser on the North in general and on the force he'd served in particular. Something of a bureaucrat by inclination, a stickler by training and a patriot by nature, Carruthers fought valiantly (and usually unsuccessfully) against studio misrepresentations. "I love the Royal Canadian Mounted Police and Canada and its people," he once wrote, "and I am idealist enough to believe that Right can win out against Greed and Ignorance." Carruthers became an unofficial liaison between the RCMP and the film-makers. He found ample opportunity to vent his righteous indignation.

The third character is Archibald Newman, the PR man who in the late 1940s and early 1950s headed something called the Canadian Co-operation Project. This body existed for the purpose of preventing the Canadian government from imposing import quotas. Part of its purpose was also to entice Hollywood producers to insert references to Canada in films not otherwise concerned with Canada. A typical result is the point in *Bend of the River*, an undistinguished Universal western, at which Jimmy Stewart looks skyward and comments, "Those are red-wing orioles from Canada." This species does not exist in Canada, or elsewhere. Such references were thought to have a favourable effect on American tourism in Canada.

If, as some critics pointed out, Berton in *The National Dream* and *The Last Spike* seemed to identify with the railway builder William Van Horne, then in *Hollywood's Canada* he identifies with Carruthers, the reformed Mountie; or at least he seems to resemble him. Berton lets pass marvellous opportunities for writing mini-essays on warring mythologies and other pop culture matters and instead concentrates on hair splitting, albeit with some pretty thick hairs. He goes through the principal Mountie pictures and finds fault with historical detail. Here in this film, he writes, the Mounties of 1883 were shown wearing stetsons when any fool knows they then wore pillboxes with chin-straps, and so on for Mountie film after Mountie film. When he comes to egregious errors of historical record in films about the Klondike, he nearly has apoplexy. It all becomes a bit tiresome after a while, the way Berton grows bitter and loud, though some of this is counterbalanced by pleasing digressions that set the record straight, digressions about how Mountie hats (stetsons, that is) are manufactured from special felt or how placer gold is mined.

Not that Berton doesn't have a wider vision as well, one that leads the reader to suggest that, although he compares favourably with Carruthers, he might better be put against no less a figure than Cecil B. DeMille himself. Although DeMille made a mess of *North West Mounted Police*, he did, in most of his films, spend enormous sums ferreting out small details of costume and locale, thinking that these would add up to some form of historic truth. He also had, in an exaggerated way, Berton's outlook on history. They have the same enthusiasm bordering on passion with which they struggle to infect their audiences. They have the same belief that history is composed of big (sometimes little-known) men caught in the throes of a continuous series of still-larger events. Drama. Big stories. That's what DeMille demanded of the writers he employed and that is what Berton aims for as well. If a cross-media comparison can be credible, Berton in his most successful writing succeeds far more than DeMille ever did at his peak form: he's more of a scholar than he is a showman, though of course far more a showman than any scholar or even any other popular historian.

An essential question of this book should be: Can Canadians or anyone else really blame the movie industry for making a farce of historical truth? The question is not only left unanswered, it's barely raised at all. The considered reply must be that, on balance, one cannot especially fault them for balling up Canada; they balled up the rest of the world as well, and in the process made what almost amounts to an alternate reality. When film approaches history, has it a responsibility to historical truth as that is generally understood? Obviously it has in one sense, in order to keep from becoming fantastic, but in another sense whatever film does becomes truth of a kind through immediacy and repetition until the film-truth is just as widely accepted as the other. If, thanks to Hollywood, much of the world still believes that Canada is a land of snow, trees and brave Mounties, it believes with equal conviction that Japan consists of pagodas, Fujiyama and men like Mr Moto, with white suits and buck-teeth.

What Hollywood did was merely to intensify preconceived notions about geography and people. If Canada's case is different it is different only on two grounds: one, persistence; two, the fact that the Hollywood stereotypes of Canadians were modifications of other film stereotypes. Hollywood's English Canadian was modified Englishman or American, its French Canadian was a modified Frenchman; only the Canadian Indian was in his natural state — but exactly like the American Indian, who was a film creation almost unto himself. Berton argues that such stereotypes were sometimes accepted as literal truth in Canada as well as in the rest of the world. As proof he cites the alacrity with which Canadians fell for Grey Owl as some legitimate embodiment of the native people. His argument is weaker than his point. The fact is that Hollywood was never much good at eradicating ignorance and bigotry but excelled at making them entertaining. In a similar way, *Hollywood's Canada*, considered in terms of all Berton's other work, is part of the struggle to create a rival mythology and to make Canadians a bit more certain of their place in the world.

Saturday Night, 1975

iii

It was perhaps too much to expect that the October Crisis should have captured the imaginations of Canadian movie-makers, a group whose imaginations are notoriously elusive. Still, it's pleasing to realize that the events of 1970 have brought out the documentary urges in at least two directors, Michel Brault, creator of *Les Ordres*, and Robin Spry, assembler of the NFB films *Action* and *Reaction*. It's pleasing and hardly unexpected. This is, after all, a nation of documentary makers, partly because of the vastness of that which is available for documentation and partly because artists and artisans here work for the government, however loudly they deny it. It is this second reason as well as the facts of the case that colour Spry's *Action*, the only one of these films so far seen by sizeable audiences in English Canada.

The present generation of Canadian directors are enlisted men or veterans of the CBC and the NFB, and this shows in large ways and small. It shows in that they have their own set of clichés. Their dew-drops always glisten in close-up. Their horses' hooves always throw mud on the Plexiglas shielding the camera below. And ah! those indiscriminate bursts of French horns and oboes. This governmental education shows, more importantly, in their very concept of film. When Don Shebib, after years of making docs and mini-docs, set out at last to do a fictional feature, how natural, how inevitable that he should have made *Goin' Down the Road*, no fiction at all but a closet documentary. It's not that these people have a social consciousness necessarily. It's that they have a governmental one. And governments are uninterested in fictions except their own official ones, such as the "apprehended insurrection" in Quebec four years ago, which Spry does a good job of reaffirming as sham.

The first thirty minutes or one-quarter of *Action* is devoted to setting the scene for the entrance of the FLQ. The groundwork is laid with such care that it seems at times as though the film, like some lesser NFB production, is aimed at the export market — which in a way it is. Although a French version of it also exists, Spry's film is clearly intended for consumption by the foreigners of English-speaking Canada. The obvious care taken to trace the base of terrorism in Quebec politics and social history is not so much an attempt to show both sides of the issue as it is an attempt to put the retrospective message across to the 85 per cent of the population who thought Pierre Trudeau correct in suspending civil liberties and throwing *ex post facto* out the window.

Action is comprised of stock footage from television stations and other sources and of film shot at the time by three NFB crews, ostensibly for archival reasons. The editing of this material into a cohesive whole is skilfully and delicately carried out, with the proper touch of light-fingered irony. Spry's way of giving everyone his due is to show everyone to have been an ass. Trudeau comes across as a knight with one fatal chink in his armour, a pathological inability to suffer fools gladly. Sensing prolonged embarrassment in the political card-game, he simply kicks over the table, uniting, for a brief time, the whole country against the radical intellectual francophones who were once his kind. Stanfield, for his part, is shown as his usual ineffectual self in moments of stress, and Diefenbaker, well, he's depicted without difficulty as a blustering gravy-stained old windbag lacking the faintest notion of what's happening.

Although treated with a deft hand, René Lévesque is also caricatured. He's shown cursing an English reporter who has asked him to confine his comments to sixty seconds but then giving his comments anyway. But because this takes place at a rally of francophones, he makes his statement in English less nearly perfect than his usual brand, if no less eloquent. Tommy Douglas of the NDP seems a voice in the wilderness, commonsensical and rational, but no more listened to than Diefenbaker. Jean Drapeau, in his turn, is pointed up as a shameless political opportunist, and a more effective one than anyone else save Trudeau. Robert Bourassa, in Spry's film, is nothing more than a sinister twit. The only persons in *Action* not made into cartoons, however correctly or deservedly, are the terrorists themselves, and this is revealing. Spry paints them neither as revolutionaries nor as punks. He could hardly be expected to, given the small amount of actual footage of them available. All he can do is to impute both interpretations. As this affects the film's audience, it's all to the good.

As it is, there is reason to believe that either the CBC or the NFB (which has a history of suppression) may be trying to keep this film from being seen nationally. Had the director — horrors — actually voiced his opinion of the FLQ it probably wouldn't even be getting as wide a distribution as it is. It's one thing to ridicule the leaders of the government and the opposition so long as you do so equally. It's quite another to treat as humans a group who are the avowed enemy of the state and the other way around. That would have made *Action* a political film, and in government eyes it's probably bad enough that this work goes beyond the documentary and into the journalistic.

It is to Spry's credit, given the system in which he works politically and artistically, that he knows just how much he can get away with and still make an important film, integrity intact. But then, remembering how much one can get away with is a skill Canadian directors display regularly. To remember or to be in the habit is to be acceptable to the backers and pleasing to the public.

Reaction, Spry's sequel to *Action*, concentrates on the effects of the early morning raids on the lives of those raided and on the lives of unmolested observers. In this it comes closest in approach to *Les Ordres*, in which Brault attempts to condense into a handful of fictional cases the experiences of some fifty detainees he interviewed. I haven't seen either film yet but await the opportunity of comparing them. Brault, it seems certain, will take a more personal and also more propagandistic approach. Partial backing by the CFDC allows for this sort of thing more easily than CBC or NFB sanction does, if only because to withhold such support would make matters worse politically, or so Ottawa must believe.

The Canadian Forum, 1975

iv

Much has happened in regard to film accounts of the October Crisis since Robin Spry's NFB documentary *Action*, an overview of that sad series of events, was reviewed in this space. The first thing that happened was that after ten months of bureaucratic stalling the CBC finally agreed to show *Action* on television. The second was the announcement that Ron Haggart will be among those working on a two-and-a-half-hour CBC retrospective of the crisis to be telecast on or near the fifth anniversary next October. The third and by far most important happening was the overdue appearance of a subtitled version of Michel Brault's *Les Ordres*, a film itself once tangled in a story of NFB and CFDC shenanigans.

The appealing aspect of Brault's film is that it is not propaganda, or at least not the political kind. Although it was written and directed by an activist non-militant *québécois*, and although it was financed partly by the CFDC and to some extent (it is reported) by the Parti Québécois, it supports no group except perhaps the people lobby. It is a thoroughly humanistic account of the inhumane treatment given those persons rounded up under the War Measures Act. Their cases have been distilled into five fictionalized stories woven together with great skill to still-greater effect.

Here, in Brault, is a director who knows exactly what effects he wants and then goes out and creates them. He can get good solid work out of his actors; for even when he has them introduce themselves at the beginning by their true names, there is, in what follows, never the least doubt that they are anything but the characters they portray. So too he can manufacture exactly the proper visual mood. As Claude Jutra's cinematographer on *Kamouraska* and *Mon Oncle Antoine* he showed what he could do with colour. Here he shows what he can do in spite of it. Putting only the prison scenes in colour was apparently a device related to the economics of the film but also, I'll wager, one intended to tell us, on reflection, just how unobtrusive good photography should be. But all this says nothing about the tremendous impact of the film, an impact created through subtlety rather than aggression.

The people in *Les Ordres* are not terrorists and neither are they sympathizers. They are ordinary folks in the black-and-white backyard of Montreal. Yet they are various. Jean Lapointe and Helene Loiselle play a mill worker active in union politics and his unpolitical wife, and Guy Provost is a physician and one-time defeated socialist candidate who runs a clinic in the slums. Claude Gauthier is an unemployed young man of still-smaller involvement but hotter temper, and the Quebec singer Louise Forestier appears as a social worker imprisoned along with the unionist-labourer's wife.

The composite story concerns these characters' backgrounds less than it concerns their doubt and anxiety in prison, cut off from their families for they don't know how long and cut off also from the larger events unfolding outside. Their pasts are used only to show their innocence and the abruptness and senselessness of their incarceration. The story from then on is the maltreatment and worry they endured while the rest of us talked, signed petitions and wrote essays about the police tactics which to them, at first hand, were vastly more grotesque.

A large measure of the tremendous pull of *Les Ordres* is tied up in the relationship between film and contemporary history. Since the audience remembers clearly the events leading to these jailings, and remembers also perhaps the stories of the actual internments from which these ones are drawn, since in short it is all so close to home, there is more audience involvement than there is in the usual documentary. And there is audience curiosity, too — about just how bad the prisons were, for instance (they were physically excellent by international standards, it appears from *Les Ordres*, but psychologically worse than the norm).

Because the audience knows how the story turns out yet cannot help become caught up with these characters, there is a tendency for the viewer's emotions to run ahead of the characters' in a way that is unusual. When

Gauthier is told he is going to be executed by the guards, we see him led to an underground garage and shot — with blank cartridges, he realizes when he recovers from his faint. Watching this, we of course know that he was not murdered. If one's murder is not reported in the Toronto *Sun*, one may be presumed alive. Yet we feel a combination of the bitterness and shock he feels after the fact and of suspense concurrent with the action on the screen. Throughout the film, the watchers and the actors interact this way. It is somewhat like good theatre, and the effect is disquieting.

Meanwhile, other films on the October Crisis are being planned and still others that have been completed have yet to be shown commercially across the country. At this writing, the solicitor Aubrey Golden, co-author with Haggart of the book *Rumours of War*, is said to be negotiating with CTV in connection with that network's own television special for the fifth anniversary. Yet *Reaction*, Robin Spry's codicil to *Action*, so far has been seen here only on the level of community groups. Jean-Claude Lord's *Bingo*, said to be a more fictionalized treatment of the prisoners than Brault's film, has scarcely been shown publicly at all outside Quebec.

The Canadian Forum, 1975

V

Unlike the publicity campaign surrounding it, Murray Markowitz's *Recommendation for Mercy* is a film that goes out of its way to avoid sensationalism. This is why it fails both as cinematic art and as social criticism. The film is partly based on and partly extrapolated from the famous Steven Truscott murder case, a scandal that stirs emotions in Ontario even now and has the potential for greater and wider controversy.

Markowitz apparently decided to make a film that everyone could agree with or that at least no one could disagree with violently. Such a tactic can be written off as a kind of sensationalism in itself and thus a commercial ploy. This view cannot be discounted if one remembers that Markowitz made *August & July*, the 1972 lesbian sexploitation film. But it could also be said that *Recommendation for Mercy* is in the public service tradition of those U.S. television specials on gun control or busing, which suggest all possible alternatives and allow the viewers to decide for themselves. Logically considered, though, only one thing about *Recommendation for Mercy* is certain: that it is a very muddled film.

Press reports indicate that Markowitz had to walk a narrow path to avoid litigation from Truscott himself and from a couple of earlier writers on the subject. Such threats, however, seem only to have italicized Markowitz's original intention of taking sides neither on Truscott's innocence or guilt nor on related questions of greater importance and timeliness. The result is that this is not a muck-raking film. It's not even a shit-disturbing film. It's more like a Rorschach test for audiences. Those who believe Truscott should have been hanged sixteen years ago, and even those who believe Solicitor General Warren Allmand should be hanged now for his stand against capital punishment, will find here fuel for their opinions. So will persons who think Truscott was innocent. So in fact will persons on both sides of such issues as judicial reform, pornography and police brutality. This film agrees with no one but incites everyone — the pro-abortionists and the anti-abortionists, the rapists and the victims — everyone. It thus has broad social appeal, just as pap has broad escapist appeal.

Truscott, for the few who need their memories refreshed, was fourteen years old when he was sentenced to hang, in 1959, for the rape-murder of thirteen-year-old Lynne Harper near Clinton, Ontario. The sentence created a furore at the time, when hangings in Ontario, though infrequent, were still allowed to take place. It inspired many editorialists and commentators, Pierre Berton not the least of them, to some of their finest hours. At length, the sentence was commuted to life imprisonment, largely because of the prisoner's youth.

In 1966 a writer named Isabel LeBourdais appeared from nowhere with a book entitled *The Trial of Steven Truscott* (she has since become an activist for senior citizens' rights). Her book argued that the evidence against him had been circumstantial and inconclusive and urged a new trial. The issue went to the Supreme Court of Canada, which upheld the conviction and sentence in an eight-to-one decision. A couple of years later, in 1969, Truscott was paroled, at age twenty-four. He's now married, with children, and lives under an assumed name in the Guelph area. With Bill Trent, then a writer for *Weekend* magazine, he later wrote his own book, *The Steven Truscott Story*. The next year Hugh Garner published *A Nice Place to Visit*, a novel inspired by the case.

Garner's novel, which concerned a broken-down journalist who years later comes upon the truth of what really happened, has at least one element in common with Markowitz's film, the view that small Ontario communities are invidious by nature. The novel was most emphatic on this point and in fact created an evil aura. Markowitz's script (written with Fabian Jennings and Joel Weisenfeld) is less stylized and less original. It shows, among other things, the willingness of witnesses to lie out of pure vindictiveness, the wont of cops to make the facts conform to simple solutions and the trick of the judge to make almost certain the jurors find in accord with his own prejudice.

This would be shocking if it weren't all a pack of clichés, the stuff of a thousand television soapers. Certainly it's not tantamount to Markowitz stating his own opinions and then trying to convince us of their validity. Even if Markowitz had taken this approach, his views would have suffered in the face of all the inaccuracies and improbabilities inherent in the script. He seems, for instance, never to have set foot inside a Canadian courtroom during business hours; his ideas on Canadian jurisprudence owe much to the movies about the Old Bailey. Which is not to say that he stands a safe distance from the story. On the contrary, he does involve himself in the film, but he's careful to confuse us with a welter of uncertainties. His approach reminds me of that passage in Sinclair Lewis's *The Man Who Knew Coolidge*, wherein one of the characters is said to have studied carefully all sides of the question and then and only then to have gone off half cocked.

Recommendation for Mercy, which is set in 1970, is full of cheap shots. Not in the technical sense, for two or three scenes are beautifully constructed, though the cinematography is poor considering the source: Richard Leiterman. Rather, the film is lazy dramatically as well as journalistically. Markowitz starts out with two unknowns, Andrew Skidd and Michele Fansett, in the Truscott- and Harper-inspired roles. Skidd has a fresh, frightened-deer face, and he is perfectly convincing in the scenes preceding his arrest. To have been more than convincing — to have been memorable — in the scenes of his incarceration and trial would have required a virtuoso performance. The failure to lead an amateur even to attempt such a performance (presupposing that he has it in him) is curious. In this case, I suspect, it can be partly explained by the director's dread of giving the audience a figure either too sympathetic or too reprehensible, depending upon one's like or dislike of frightened deer in the throes of malfeasance.

In the scene in which the prisoner is interrogated by the local police, Skidd breaks down under the pressure and lapses into an hallucination, which is indicated by a tangle of voice-overs and reverberation. This is one of the great film clichés of our time, rapidly supplanting the falling calendar leaves that indicate the passage of time and the rolling presses forecasting a scandalous newspaper headline. It is also a substitute for directing masquerading as a substitute for acting. In *Recommendation for Mercy*, however, this is one of the subtler cop-outs. The blatant, grating ones are, first, a badly done nightmare scene in which Skidd undergoes a mock execution and, second, the sheer superfluity of suspects. There are four possible killers in this case besides Skidd: two of his schoolmates, an unidentified hunter and a soldier in a red automobile. In flashbacks we are shown all five of these people committing the crime, though we are shown evidence that would tend to implicate only three of them. What's worse is that at the end of the film Skidd, in prison now five years, makes application for parole in the form of a soliloquy in which he virtually confesses his guilt and repents.

Is this meant to tell us that the corrupt system has now corrupted him into lying in exchange for freedom? Or is this just poor film-making? I tend to think it is the latter. *Recommendation for Mercy* tries blurring the distinctions between fiction and documentary, between statement and stimulus, but with little success. Still, one should not come down too hard on Markowitz or his movie, for it is an important piece of work worthy of some discussion. It is merely that the discussion leads to the conclusion that

Markowitz's main fault is that he lacks the faults of Costa-Gavras and Emile de Antonio. He has no point of view. Perhaps the best thing to be said of *Recommendation for Mercy* is that it is a film of absolutely no interest to Americans, who would regard it as an inept crime drama rather than an inept piece of social comment.

There is an overpowering need for this type of Canadian film-making, dealing with historical figures who, by their strength or their weakness, have touched off something in the Canadian imagination. So far, however, such figures — one thinks of the Black Donnellys, Nellie McClung, Mackenzie — have been dealt with much more frequently by the playwrights and much better too. As for Markowitz, he is certainly a director of potential consequence. The difficulty one has with his career to date, however, is the same difficulty one has with dealing with this film in particular: namely, deciding whether it's an honest attempt gone awry or merely a commercial hype. One would be inclined to say it is the former had not Markowitz announced that his next film, now in pre-production, bears striking similarities to the case of the tabloids' blessing, Peter Demeter, the Toronto man recently convicted of uxoricide.

The Canadian Forum, 1975

vi

The Heatwave Lasted Four Days, a new NFB feature directed by Doug Jackson, is not likely to be seen in Canadian cinemas, though commercial rights to it have already been assigned to other countries. It is one of five features the NFB has made to help non-native-speakers learn English, and it seems destined to live out its time in class-rooms, broken into four twenty-minute lessons, accompanied by a teachers' manual. In its unbroken form, however, it has been shown on the full CBC English network and also on ABC in the United States, not as a language aid but as an enjoyable thriller about the Montreal drug traffic. As such, it stands up remarkably well. The interest of the film, however, is that it's the clearest statement in memory of both what's wrong with the Canadian film industry as well as what's right with it. Here's all the skill and promise — and also the lassitude and anaemia — of English-Canadian cinema, all in one can. It's almost too instructive to be true.

The plot has to do with a television news cameraman, played by Gordon Pinsent. He's routinely assigned to shoot some film at a Montreal beach to illustrate a weather story. Later he's approached by one of the couples there (Larry Dane and Alexandra Stewart) who want to purchase the footage in which they appear. Dane explains the offer by saying that he fears his wife might learn he's cheating on her with his beach partner, and to the newsman this is reasonable enough at first. What develops, of course, is that Dane is no errant husband but a drug importer wanted equally by the authorities and the mob. The tension in the story results when, discovering this, Pinsent decides to hold out for more money. His demand is met, but part of the bargain is that he help in the smuggling. The whole thing ends in disaster. It's more complex than it sounds from this description, and Pinsent, a better actor than he's usually given opportunity to prove, does a journeyman's job as the avaricious smoke-chaser with a taste for crime but no stomach for it. Just how this is useful language instruction I can't imagine, but that's beside the point; so is the fact that Canadians only got an opportunity to see this film after it was well received in the States. The point is rather that the strength of the film is Pinsent, who struggles to bring life to the role and succeeds. Had it not been for him we wouldn't have been missing much.

It was nearly a decade ago that Andrew Sarris remarked, with a certain bewilderment, that Canadian films seemed to exhibit all the technical facility in the world and hardly any personality. He was right, of course, and things have not improved. What he didn't understand was why this was the case. It is this way because most Canadian film-makers aren't educated, they're trained. They receive their early training — and in some cases spend their careers — working for the NFB and the CBC. This is the great virtue of Canadian cinema but also its bane.

On one level there's much to be said for such training, of course. The NFB has sometimes led the world in animation, for instance; and there's likely no better place on earth than Jarvis Street for learning how to do things cheaply, quickly and against improbable bureaucratic odds. Such techniques, and some of them are dazzling, are the hallmarks of Canadian cinema both here and abroad. (Would those split-screen title sequences in *The Thomas Crown Affair* be so good if Norman Jewison weren't Canadian? No. They wouldn't exist at all.) Yet the fact remains that on a less technical, more imaginative level these organizations teach only how to make films, not how to create them.

Film-makers, script-writers and all the other personnel here come to believe that every film or programme must have a function beyond its visual one. This is a remnant of Orange frugality carried over into the public affairs mentality. You can't own a mere pet; it has to earn its keep as a Presbyterian watch-dog or rat-killer around the barn. In the same way you can't simply make a film. You must make a film that teaches English to Latvians or explains metric measurement or eases tensions between two provinces.

This is the System. It's journalistic rather than literary. It teaches how to pass along information but not how to deal with ideas. Each year it grows stronger, and each year wonderment increases as to why our films are the way they are. The reason is the System. It's as though all writers were forced to work at the Toronto *Star* and then we were to speculate as to why there weren't any good novelists. Coy wordsmiths? Yes. In abundance. Fast typists? In limitless supply. But novelists? Gee, what do we know about art and stuff like that?

The statement that the System is the problem breaks down into two parts, the first of which I've just had done with. The second part is that as well as neglecting aesthetic considerations for journalistic ones, the System thereby encourages a smugness which complicates the whole business. It's the smugness of the newsman over the artist, the self-assurance that comes with the knowledge that what one deals with is tangible and black and white: news copy that's either correct or incorrect, good or bad. Because the English-speaking audience is so large here (and because, as an audience, is interchangeable with one to the south ten times as large) there is nothing to counteract this smugness. There's nothing of the continual self-doubt the artist faces, aware that his raw materials are not facts at all and never can be, but impulses, inspirations, interpretations. This state of mind cannot be instilled by training, unfortunately. But it can be abetted by circumstances conducive to introspection.

For instance, the Quebec film-makers (a high percentage of whom are also System men) are generally speaking better than ours artistically because being a Quebecker forces one into a certain kind of self-appraisal. Similarly, in Australia, where the state network and film office play a part in the national life almost equal to the part ours play here, the film-makers seem to feel lost to Britain, alien to Pacific Asia and forgotten by everyone else. As a consequence, their feature films, on balance, have begun to surpass those of English Canada in artistic (rather than simply visual) content.

What all this has to do with *The Heatwave Lasted Four Days* is as follows: Our film-makers seldom think to operate outside the System. They seldom try forgetting what they've learned by rote. Their aim is not inward examination but outward comparison. Until recently this meant that we always came off second-best in the comparison. Now it means only that the smugness has increased. Once we said, "If only we could make trash as well as the Americans, then we could probably make gems as well as they do too." Now we say, "Okay, we've proved it. Our trash is every bit as good as yours but also distinctly our own, with the marks of our System on it. Pay up and let's go get looped together." I suppose that is *some* improvement but depressingly little.

The Heatwave Lasted Four Days struck me as a useful symbol. Here was a tight script, well cast, photographed with our peculiar flair and generally handled with professionalism and aplomb. It had an ulterior motive, but that's all right, I suppose, considering the source. In the last analysis, though, you can't escape the conclusion that it was a tiny film, unambitious: a tame thriller raising no questions, affirming nothing, denying nothing, telling us nothing of actual human beings and how they behave. It's a symbol because, unless I'm badly mistaken, this is as far as we can go under the System as it's presently constituted. There are only three choices. We can slip backwards into "You show me your trash, I'll show you mine." We can stay as we are, making slight improvements perhaps, but mainly polishing the knob on a locked and bolted door. Or we can change the System.

The Canadian Forum, 1975

vii

The curious thing about *Russian Roulette,* the American film starring George Segal, is that it's much more realistically Canadian than Tom Ardies's *Kosygin Is Coming,* the Canadian novel on which it's based. In this respect it may very well be unique. On those infrequent occasions in the past when Americans made films from Canadian books, they tended to de-Canadianize them drastically if not entirely. Similarly, when Americans shoot films in Canada for financial reasons they more often than not disguise the location so that it resembles the United States as much as possible; and of course American movies of the past (*Rose Marie, Saskatchewan* and so on) were notorious for making Canada and Canadians seem all rather too British.

Russian Roulette is interesting for tossing these precedents aside. Here we have an American film made in Vancouver and clearly labelling itself as such. Here we have Segal as an RCMP officer who behaves and speaks more like a Canadian than an American or a Briton. This is in contrast with the original book, in which the characters major and minor speak and think like Englishmen, calling one another "bloke" and, in one instance, even resorting to "blimey." In the film much of this nonsense is toned down. If anything, the Canadianness is exaggerated.

Although the credits attribute the screenplay to Ardies himself, Stanley Mann and Arnold Margolin, it is difficult to determine how accurate an indication this is of who did the writing, since credit is frequently called for by contract when there is little or no basis for such credit in fact. Whatever the true proportions of the collaboration in this case, one thing is certain: the script is just what an adapted screenplay should be, a much-improved version of the book. Indeed, *Russian Roulette* is less a mere adaptation of Ardies's 1974 thriller than it is a valuable rewrite of it in a different medium. Few writers (let alone Canadian ones) ever have such an opportunity for correcting their mistakes; Ardies, with however much help from Mann and Margolin, has made the best of it.

The plot has its factual basis in Soviet Premier Aleksei Kosygin's troubled tour of Canada in 1970. The story, in brief, is that of Corporal Timothy Shaver. After fifteen years with the RCMP he's been suspended for striking his commanding officer. Shortly before Kosygin is due in Vancouver, he's contacted by a man named Petapiece, an officer of the Special Branch (which even then was actually called the Security Service). Petapiece wants Shaver to kidnap a man named Henke, an East European trouble-maker the Russians want safely out of the way until the visit is over. Petapiece makes clear that if the mission is completed successfully he will put in the fix with the force so that Shaver will be reinstated.

Two days before the visit Shaver discovers that a party or parties unknown have already kidnapped Henke or possibly murdered him and disposed of the body. Rather than report this and render his dismissal a foregone conclusion, he decides to try to rekidnap Henke himself in the forty-eight hours remaining. In the course of this attempt, he kills a syndicate torpedo from Detroit hired to get the Mountie out of the way. Later he learns that Henke is in fact an employee of the CIA.

The conspiracy unfolds something like this: Some members of the KGB, fearful of *détente* between the Soviets and the Americans of which this Canadian tour is an early step, are planning to assassinate Kosygin themselves; it's they who are holding Henke, whom they intend to make into a human bomb and drop from a helicopter onto the official motorcade; the reasoning is that the two superpowers will plunge back into cold war once a CIA man — one the Canadians have been asked to immobilize — kills the Russian leader on Canadian soil with Canadian aid or at least through Canadian incompetence.

Shaver, acting alone, learns all this. At the very last moment, he shoots down the helicopter and kills its passenger before anyone can detonate the explosives. This follows a gun battle on the oxydized copper roof of the Hotel Vancouver. Such are the story elements common to both the book and the film. The discrepancies in the two entertainments provide an unusual opportunity for examining the differences between Hollywood's idea of Canada and Canada's idea of Hollywood.

Ardies, who is a practised thriller writer, makes a number of concessions to the genre's traditions. One of the laws of the thriller is that the author must have enough inside information about various specialized occupations and situations to make them believeable to his reader but not enough to contradict the reader's preconceived ideas. For instance, Shaver, at one point when he's on Henke's trail (the scene is dropped in the film), poses as a newspaperman and carries on about the profession with a bus driver. The view he gives is all wrong. The driver doesn't know this of course and neither does the reader. But Ardies himself must know, since he's a former Vancouver *Sun* reporter.

Similarly, the novel, as already mentioned, contains some of the most British dialogue since Len Deighton. Yet Shaver himself sometimes breaks from talking like a music-hall performer in order to speak like a flippant, slangy American private detective. When he's forcing information out of the hit man on a bridge above the Fraser River (a scene recorded in the film as well as in the novel) he tells the man to "fink or swim." It's like something Lew Archer or Philip Marlowe would say. Coming from a Mountie, who should talk more like a bureaucrat than a baseball player, it sounds wrong. The tough thriller is an American-dominated form, and Ardies goes along with these facts of life.

It's as though Ardies had his eye on an American movie sale all along. If so, this explains why his characters are so British, because in the past Hollywood has usually liked its English-speaking Canadians to be that way. In this case, however, Hollywood had come nearer the truth than before by discarding all the come-ons, or most of them, while concentrating, perhaps too much, on true-to-life Canadiana. There are several close shots of beer bottles that emphasize the funny labels on the BC brands. Another shot shows Shaver jimmying a lock with a Chargex card rather than with one of the American credit cards.

The film is directed by Lou Lombardo, who was formerly Robert Altman's editor, a modest enough claim to fame. Here, together with his screen-writers, he has made great improvements on the original material. They have tightened up the action, which in the book moves slowly until the final chapters. They have discarded many superfluous characters and situations. They have changed the corny ending of the book wherein Shaver and his RCMP girl-friend decide to get married. What he, or they, have made in fact is not only a better movie that the book is a book but also a hybrid film that is half Canadian and half American.

The film lacks the glossiness that would have attached to an American thriller shot in the States. But because it apparently used Canadians behind the scenes, it displays one of the great strengths of Canadian film, the ability to capture the essence of a geographical place in an almost impressionistic manner. The city of Vancouver in Lombardo's film (like the city of Montreal in *The Pyx*) looks absolutely true to itself. Taking in the cinematography one says to oneself, yes, that's exactly the way Vancouver feels and smells; that's precisely the amount of space things have around them out there in the winter. This holds true mainly for the scenes of the city itself but it also applies to those shot at Grouse Mountain (which do not occur in the book).

More importantly, the film is pleasing to the sensibilities of both nations because of the way it depicts cops. The RCMP shown here are sufficiently corrupt to ring true to the American audience's view of cops everywhere yet wholesome and clean-cut enough to allow Canadians to retain their naïve pride in their own federal police. If the film shows times to have changed at all in police circles, it's American time and not Canadian. In the film, the fellow who has come from Detroit to bump off Shaver is a hit man, nothing more, nothing less. In the book, however, this character too has CIA connections. Perhaps when the film was being planned, it was thought this angle would have been too much for the Americans to swallow, but not so now. Canadians of course still believe such things don't happen on Canadian soil no matter who is behind them. The Canadianness of this film has won out.

Books in Canada, 1975

viii

If one were to put the point of Peter Pearson's telefilm *The Insurance Man From Ingersoll* in one sentence, that sentence would go like this: "It's pointless trying to prove the truth; yet merely stating the truth, without proof, makes one party to the lie." This film, part of the CBC *Performance* series, concerns unethical relationships between government and private enterprise. It's about the shady deals the media never quite pin down because the media are too much a part of the power structure such stories would jeopardize. It's about the kind of deal we all suspect takes place and suspect so strenuously that it becomes, in our minds, an accepted fact — which unfortunately is not the same as accepted truth. *The Insurance Man From Ingersoll* is very good at capturing the feeling of frustration this state of affairs brings on. It's also good at capturing the mood of one level of Toronto powermongering. It walks close to the edge, cuts close to the bone. It's a fine example of what television should be used for but almost never is. Whether it will provoke anyone enough to take the message seriously is quite a different matter. The defeat of public spirit the film depicts breeds not fury but increased dejection and apathy. The film may merely reinforce the belief that the truth is out there, somewhere, but cannot be proved.

A pseudo-investigative television journalist of the Carole Taylor stripe (Charlotte Blunt) uncovers irregularities and violence in a Toronto construction union. The workers who are being short-changed, and roughed up if they object, are erecting a huge high-rise office complex. This leads the journalist's lover, an avenging MPP played by Michael Magee, to try getting to the bottom of what promises to be a first-rate scandal. What lies at the bottom (and what the provincial member never quite succeeds in making public) is that the developer has leased several floors to the government even before the ground was broken. The lease was so long and exorbitant as to pay for the building, in effect, before it was begun. In pre-arranged gratitude, the developer then kicks back $100,000 to the party in power. The party thus gets a hundred grand; the developer has a free building; and nearly everyone is happy. The only unhappy one is the crusading MPP, who appeals to the provincial attorney general for help, unaware that he too is involved; that indeed the conspiracy extends to the premier, who is coyly referred to throughout only as "the Old Man." In the end, this (to the conspirators) unwarranted interference from Magee and the media results in the title character, a political fixer and bagman, forcing the attorney general to resign for the sake of appearances. The big villains have sacrificed the lesser villain (who is also a nice guy) to protect themselves.

It's a very Toronto story. Toronto after all is a place whose social, economic and political history for the past thirty years has been the transference of power from old Scottish gangsters to new indigenous gangsters, a process that's often been mistaken for progress. For Toronto viewers the film will have special relevance because the spirit and the implication are true to life and also because the film is, to some extent, a *pièce à clef*. At least some of the characters are recognizable composites of public personalities and some of the events (though not the key ones) are inspired by stories still fresh in the mind.

For example, Michael Magee as Edward Blake is clearly intended to represent Morton Shulman in his career as NDP member for High Park. (Shulman's earlier career, as Metro Toronto coroner, formed the basis for the *Wojeck* series of several years ago.) And of course the name of the character, Edward Blake, is a somewhat hallowed one, that of the nineteenth-century Liberal leader who never quite became prime minister. The actual Shulman, it should be said, has never lacked ambition or flair, though Pearson, like the *Wojeck* producers, plays down Shulman's flamboyance and talent for publicity. Indeed, Magee makes his character flat and almost totally devoid of endearing qualities save earnestness, a sort of Ralph Nader figure.

As for the other characters, Ramsay, the attorney general, seems to be rooted in the Conservative cabinet minister Dalton Bales, who has had dramatic and somewhat silly run-ins with Shulman. But David Gardner, the actor playing Ramsay, bears more than a good resemblance to Darcy McKeogh, who has also held cabinet posts under Tory Premier Bill Davis. The title character is portrayed by Warren Davis, the veteran CBC staff announcer, a brilliant stroke of casting on Pearson's part. Even though Davis is awkward in some of his delivery, it is only natural that a man who once read the national news should make a convincing heavy. This character, who we're led to believe was a crony of the premier's in their home district, doesn't actually correspond to anyone in the present government, but suggests the London, Ontario, advisers and hangers-on who cultivated and were cultivated by the Conservative Premier John Robarts, a native of that city.

This precise type of composite, which allows Pearson to get away with an incredible amount of sensitive muck-raking for CBC, is present throughout the film in another way. It is used heavily in the plot, for which credit must go to Norman Hartley, who shares writing credit with the director. The simple truth is that there have been no scandals in the Ontario government similar in dimension to those in the film since the days of Leslie Frost. Such scandals as do surface are usually broken by the press (lately by *The Globe and Mail*, where Hartley is a reporter) and almost never by members of the legislature. *The Insurance Man From Ingersoll* does avail itself, however, of two recent foofooraws. The first centred on the fact that a friend of the premier's had been given the edge in bidding on the new Ontario Hydro building. In the end little damage was done to anyone; anyway, it was proved that the taxpayer was still getting reasonable value for his money. In the second and rather more complicated scandal, it was learned that another developer, a friend of several ministers, made sizeable donations to the party after Cabinet had passed on a government contract awarded him. Crown attorneys investigated but found no grounds for charges.

The important fact, however, is that the film works this tissue of actuality into what passes quite convincingly for the whole cloth. There is even a sub-plot involving organized crime, a subject dear to Ontario editorialists. This sub-plot also helps make the Blake-Shulman connection. Shulman once made accusations resulting in a contract on his life and then went about for weeks packing a side-arm. What's more, even though Pearson was not able to film in the legislative chamber itself, he has skilfully used other locations — the actual apartment blocks, the perfect streetcorners — where such devious and quintessentially Toronto action would, and undoubtedly does, take place.

In one way the film is true to the course of Pearson's career to date since it concerns a rebel thwarted by the dominant society, a theme that pre-dates *Paperback Hero* and goes back to his NFB documentary on Saul Alinsky. But in another sense, *The Insurance Man From Ingersoll* is a breakthrough and should be taken notice of as such. It's a convincing thriller and non-violent gangster film — more importantly, a political thriller and an upper-middle-class gangster film. It's thus a fine piece of folk art for Toronto, a place that in film, as in life, has hitherto always taken a back seat to Montreal in these matters.

Cinema Canada, 1976

ix

In Jan Kadar's film *Lies My Father Told Me* there is a supporting character named Mr. Bumgarten, who operates a small tailor shop in Montreal in the 1920s. He is also the neighbourhood communist. Unlike most of the other characters in the film, Bumgarten knows the way out of the ghetto or believes he does. As a communist he simply foresees the elimination of all such slums when workers take control of the state. He proselytizes once or twice but none of the others pays much attention to him. The interesting aspect of all this is that the character is played by Ted Allan.

Allan is not only the author of the screenplay and of the short story from which it's taken, he's also one of Canada's best-known communists, the co-author of *The Scalpel, The Sword*, the biography of Norman Bethune, his one-time comrade in the Spanish Civil War. Viewed at a distance this is all richly ironic since, as a writer at least, Allan is not much for following communist doctrine. His production is geared for maximum profit rather than use, as can be seen from the history of *Lies My Father Told Me* in its several forms. The latest is the "novelization" by Norman Allan of his father's screenplay, which illustrates that Ted Allan is not above achieving the capitalist ideal of keeping his property in the family.

The original story, written nearly thirty years ago, set the pattern for everything that followed. It was a sentimental little tale, clearly autobiographical, about a young boy's attachment to his grandfather and also to the broken-down horse that pulled his grandfather's junk wagon. What develops is the child's loss of innocence, which comes about in a double brush with mortality. First the grandfather dies; then the horse, which has been the subject of complaints from the neighbours, is sold and put to death. It's a plot notable not for its substance but for its telling, and the telling has changed considerably over the years.

Also integral to the story are the boy's mother and father. In the original, the latter was a nebulous sort of character. But in 1954, when Allan converted the story into a CBC-TV script, which he subsequently sold in a number of other countries as well, the parent became more clearly defined. He was now a successful man of business who supported his family without too much strain. His residence in the ghetto, it seemed, was more a matter of ethnic ties than of penury. This is in contrast with the film version, in which the same character, well played by Len Birman, is a gambler and a believer in crackpot inventions. Here he resents the grandfather, not only because the grandfather is closer to the boy than he is, but also because he must keep borrowing money from him.

But it is the grandfather who undergoes the more interesting change. In the original story and in the TV play, he was not the lovable wise old man he is in the film but a stern authoritarian figure, a fact that made his grandson's admiration a little harder to figure out. The television version also featured a grandmother, a superfluous character dropped from the film. Neither the story nor the two dramatic versions contained a Bumgarten or anyone like him, perhaps because communists were lying low in 1954, even in fiction. Or, more probably, because Allan only later conceived the notion of including a figure who is himself in adulthood as much as the grandson is himself when young and thus of providing, in his own mind at least, a cyclical effect.

What is important, though, is that in the film both the grandfather, who was formerly so strident, and the communist, who once would have been depicted as threatening, are both laundered. They are both made to seem, in a word, cute. This is in keeping with the white middle-class idea that radicals, foreigners and other riff-raff can be made harmless by being made the object of gentle levity. If you can't assimilate 'em, distort 'em. This fact only contributes to the feeling that *Lies My Father Told Me* has the depth of a Disney picture. If one watches it critically, in the light of Kadar's Czech films such as *The Shop on Main Street*, one succumbs to the same sort of pity one feels watching the westerns Fritz Lang made after moving from Germany to Hollywood.

That's if one watches it critically *and* in a cosmopolitan frame of mind. Watching it as a Canadian one is confronted with the double standard so troublesome for critics and audiences. One turns off one's mind and concedes that, yes, it's a well-constructed film, with good if postcardy cinematography and some fine performances. One ends up saying that at least it will have a good effect on the perpetually anaemic Canadian film industry and therefore can't be all bad. This is where Norman Allan's novelization of the screenplay comes in.

Viewed from the standpoint of the ephemera that feature films leave behind them — novelizations and sound-track albums — Canadian cinema has never been healthier. That is to say that the producers are becoming a bit more acute. By acting as though the atmosphere were lush for Canadian films, they are forming a mental attitude more deceptive to that eventuality. They are also, of course, making a few bucks on the side for all concerned.

Books in Canada, 1976

X

Lies, an hour-long documentary by Jonathon Reid and Peter Walsh about the making of Jan Kadar's *Lies My Father Told Me*, is not exactly an ambiguous film but it does demand a certain ambivalence of the audience. Or perhaps it's better to say that it is a compromise film. It is not a complete meal in itself since it doesn't show enough of the process of film-making; one doesn't have to have seen and enjoyed *Lies My Father Told Me* to appreciate it, though that would help. But neither is it a concession to those who insist on finding the ephemera of art more important than the art object. The film purports to tell the story of the making of one movie but shows only what it was like on the set, without mention of, for instance, the financial crises which beset Canadian films generally and that one especially.

Yet in an odd way *Lies* does concern itself with what in Canadian film are the twin processes of creation and survival (but, again, without any hint of the inevitable sibling rivalry). It is, then, that most difficult of all documentaries to make, the kind about an abstract idea. It's a type which Canadians, despite the overwhelming strength of the documentary tradition, have never quite been able to pull off. *Lies*, like others before it, seeks to explore a concept but leaves behind it only a mood.

Kadar himself is the star of the film, more than he was the auteur of the original one. He plays the part of the temperamental European director, a bit of type-casting if ever there was one. We see him in his fisherman's vest, pleading with, imploring, instructing and — well, directing his cast, whom he treats lovingly and harshly by turns. Tempers, as they say in *TV Guide* synopses, flare. But we know that even these flare-ups are part of his Otto Preminger act. Just as *Lies* gives us the basic plot of the original film, stripped of all the sentimental balderdash, so Kadar gives a better performance than most of his charges did in *Lies My Father Told Me*.

The film centres on behind the scenes relationships but also deals with the more interesting relationship of the actor to his task. There are interviews with the principals, including Len Birman, Marilyn Lightstone and Jeffrey Lunas, the child actor who is even more insufferable here than in the original feature. There are also appearances by Ted Allan, author of the story and the screenplay, who worked on location as dialogue coach, at Kadar's request, mainly because of the latter's difficulties with English. Except for Lightstone, a generally superior actress and, judging from this, a woman of common sense, all of the cast speak a great deal of nonsense about Art. A particularly bad moment comes when Allan, who had a small part in the film, says of Kadar: "He's really one of the best directors I've ever worked with." That is rather on the order of Arnold Bennett's remark that he really didn't agree with Einstein's theory of relativity.

What it comes down to in the end is Kadar's superior knowledge of film (momentarily prostituted in *Lies My Father Told Me*) — a knowledge that includes a knowledge of acting greater than his cast's. This, at least, the present film illustrates beautifully, without any ambiguity at all. Most of the people in this film seem very conscious of being filmed; several of them in fact are even acutely nervous about the presence of the camera. Kadar is the only one who is conscious of it though, without being self-conscious. He keeps the lens in mind but his thoughts are really on the screen

Perhaps it is inevitable (one says this with a sigh) that the story of the making of *Lies* is just as complicated as that of *Lies My Father Told Me*. The latter began shooting in Montreal in summer 1972. Reid and Walsh spent six weeks, from October to December, shooting the shooting with the intention of making a half-hour documentary. The rushes, though encouraged them, in November, to try for a full hour instead. The next month, however, the feature ground to a halt amid financial problems, taking the auxiliary project down with it.

In 1974 Kadar's people somehow found money not only to resume shooting an important scene (an expensive proposition at that point) but also to subsidize the documentary: a rare instance of the grant-getter acting as subcontractor. Despite this, the documentary still wasn't done by the time the feature was completed and released last year. Meanwhile, the documentary group had been scrounging funds wherever it could, a process that continued until February this year, when a Toronto production house took over, in effect, the whole messy project. The result is just now being released, more than three years after it was filmed and long after the appearance of the feature it depicts.

All this leads to the inescapable thought (I almost hate to say it) that there remains to be done a film of the *making* of the film *about* the making of the film. At least that is one way to look at it. Another is to say that, whereas there is now a fad in American cinemas for old trailers, here are we, one step ahead. We're actually making trailers after the fact for films that got made years earlier and then only by the skin of someone's teeth.

The Canadian Forum, 1976

xi

Joyce Wieland's *The Far Shore*, her first feature, has been one of the most eagerly awaited Canadian films of recent years. When in pre-production, and later when it was actually being made, it was given a great deal of press. The coverage was not, however, the carefully manufactured kind many films receive but sprang from an unusually sincere interest on the part of the media. The film has been advertised mostly by word of mouth, and here was an instance of the word spreading even to the magazines and newspapers. That is an unusual occurrence but then *The Far Shore* is a most unusual film. In a time when Canadian films are either sloppy exploitations of traditional Hollywood genres or slick nostalgias like *The Apprenticeship of Duddy Kravitz* and *Lies My Father Told Me*, here is a film that, in Canadian terms, makes its own genre, disregarding sloppiness and slickness for a quiet integrity all its own.

The blow by blow publicity (both printed and oral) has also been unusual in that it actually shed light on how the film evolved in the five years it took Wieland to get it written, financed and shot. It originated as a dramatization of events in the life of Tom Thomson. Legal complications, however, made it necessary to disguise the fact. The result is a character named Tom McLeod. We see him in 1919, when Thomson was already dead, as a veteran of the Canadian Expeditionary Force, which Thomson wasn't. He lives in a rustic shack in northern Ontario and paints landscapes. That, however, is one of the less important shifts in the story-line of this carefully digested and calmly laid out film.

So far as I am aware, Wieland was, about eight years ago, the first Canadian artist to state flatly that there is both female art and male art and that they are separate and distinct — neither complementary nor contradictory, just different. It seems odd, for the idea is so generally accepted today. What makes *The Far Shore* important in this context is that it is an example of female cinematic art made with discipline for a mass audience. It is disciplined in the sense that it is free of the self-indulgent brooding that the detractors of female art take to be its hallmark. It's for a mass audience in that it's a simple narrative film with all the traditional virtues of such and none of the elements common to the short experimental films Wieland has been making for about fifteen years. Judging by the piecemeal reports of the past few years, it is now more overtly a woman's film than had been originally planned.

The film opens by establishing the circumstances of a young *québécoise* named Eulalie (Céline Lomez), who is a sensitive creature without being neurotic about it. She lives in a rural Quebec of great natural beauty and practically no cultural excitement. That only heightens her melancholy and her sense of being an outsider. When a seemingly urbane and cultured mining engineer (Lawrence Benedict) arrives from English Canada, she takes a tumble for him. He is not only a companion in frustration, he's a ticket to the outside world. They marry and move to his Toronto mansion, with summers at his northern lodge.

What develops is that Eulalie has seen in the man only a romantic fantasy. In truth he's no understanding helpmate but a Philistine of some distinction. Benedict does a good job of realizing this professional man with a lawyer's money and only a lawyer's mind; and Wieland and her screen-writer, Bryan Barney, add some nice touches. For instance, when the subject turns to music, which remains Eulalie's only means of expression and consolation, he begins singing a crass music-hall ditty, "I'm the Man Who Broke the Bank at Monte Carlo." As sung by Peter O'Toole in David Lean's *Lawrence of Arabia*, the song made the point that the young Lawrence, still more adventurer than hero, was the right sort of chap: the proper combination of vicarious bounder and racist snob. In other words, it was used to show that he was the kind of Englishman he at that point actually was. Here the song has a similar function in showing that Eulalie's husband is a vapid colonial with pretensions to being an Englishman of sorts. He reeks of Osgoode Hall, the Albany Club and the *Mail and Empire* as surely as Lawrence, in the early scenes, was meant to reek of some place like Sandhurst.

It is at the summer cottage that Eulalie's husband introduces her to McLeod (Frank Moore), the quiet and clear-eyed young landscape artist. When Eulalie admires one of his canvases, the husband reveals his ignorance by suggesting that it must be more expensive than smaller ones merely because it's bigger. His condescending attitude towards McLeod is made all the more patronizing by the mock camaraderie with which he tries disguising it. Eulalie senses her mistake in marrying such a clod and does a trampoline act for Tom. They seem to understand each other instinctually. In his eyes is appreciation of her unrealized need for artistic gratification; in hers, an understanding of his tolerance of a society composed of people like her husband. They become lovers.

The engineer seems oblivious to his wife's emotional predicament. It is only when she and the artist run off together, paddling across a chain of glassy lakes, that something in him — probably a combination of masculine ego and belief in property rights — is awakened. With a buddy named Cluny (whose name bespeaks Wieland's euphonism) he tracks them down and shoots them both dead. Tom's bloody head, Eulalie's summer hat, their overturned canoe linger on the water like Yeats's long-legged fly. Cluny is aroused by the smell of blood; his friend is moved by his own passionlessness.

As already stated, in the original treatment McLeod was to have been the dominant character. It was only later, and slowly, that Eulalie rose to her full dramatic height and eclipsed both him and the husband. The result is that she at first seems to be the heroine of the film as well as the pivot. But it would be mistaken to say that all the male characters are caricatures and worse. In truth, the husband and his friend are more representatives of their class and culture than symbols of their gender. Tom, for his part, is the other side of the husband. He's another of Eulalie's fantasies, a more demanding, indeed fatal one, placed on a pedestal. Yet it's true that all this only strengthens the Eulalie character. It does not necessarily, though, make her an ideal. She is, after all, the embodiment of those annoying people who never know what they want to do with their lives and who contrive to put the blame, and the hope, on others around them.

Another behind the scenes titbit about *The Far Shore* is the fact that Wieland planned the whole feature over a period of two years on storyboards, as one would do for an animated film. That, combined with the increasing concern with landscape in her graphic art, gives the film an unusual aspect. There is about the photography little of the Kodachrome splashiness that in other films is often used as a crutch and is sometimes made a star. Yet the northern locations make three-dimensional many of the scenes, which are, like a cartoonist's or a soap opera writer's, comprised of head-and-shoulder panels in series.

The Canadian Forum, 1976

xii

For many years (it seems like many years) we have been decrying the fact that so many opportunities for English-Canadian features have been wasted. The attitude, unhealthy in its pessimism, has been that the few chances given us by God (He seems to be implicated) are precious, sacred almost. Sadness and anger result from the number of times we have been content with poorly made pieces of formulaic trash. Investors, who are pragmatic people, have opted more often for imitation American slicks than for such films as *Goin' Down the Road* or *The Far Shore*. Directors and writers, who are supposed to be artists of sorts, have usually sensed the direction of the wind. They have followed their critical successes with commercial movies in no way concerned with the lives of actual Canadians in the real Canada. It's stating too much to say that the pattern is beginning to change. But a comparison of the two new Canadian thrillers indicates that, just possibly . . . maybe the twinge of joy ought to be suppressed. Perhaps caution should prevail.

The first film is *Death Weekend*. Written and directed by William Fruet, it is a far cry from his *Wedding in White*. The producer is Ivan Reitman, who earlier gave the world *The Parasite Murders* (discreetly retitled *Shivers*) and that charming little pastiche *Cannibal Girls*. It is an outstanding example of the Old Trash. The other film is *The Clown Murders*, written and directed by Martyn Burke: an example of the New Trash which, whatever else it is, is better than the other kind and more nearly our own.

Death Weekend has all the earmarks of Canadian cinema *manqué*. There are the second-rank American stars, Don Stroud and Brenda Vaccaro. There is the amorphousness of setting: such films always take place in a North America that, despite the clues found on car licence plates, is neither one country nor the other. Finally, there is the second-generation rip-off script, exploiting all the American exploitation films. The plot basically revolves around Vaccaro's successful attempt to track down and snuff out the rowdies who have terrorized her Thanksgiving holiday. By nature a peaceful person, she has been reduced to the bestial level of her tormentors. Shades of *Death Wish*, *Straw Dogs* and probably others. The production values are high enough, but the film lacks the energy and authenticity of the originals. It raises again the hoary question: Why make such a thing? Surely no one would ever try to duplicate the chili dog or the Chicago Commodities Exchange except as parody, so why try duplicating Sam Peckinpah — and fail? One should have the real thing when one's in the mood for it. The bogus product can't be taken seriously as Canadian culture.

Such is the Old Trash. The New Trash would seem to have more to recommend it, though that statement is based solely on *The Clown Murders*, the only example of the New so far as I'm aware. In place of geographical and social indifference it has an almost bicultural aspect. Burke has not made the Canadian setting seem cute and somewhat exotic, as an American director would have done, but neither does he intend the film to be primarily for Canadians. He has presented the setting offhandedly so that Canada's profile is neither high nor low. There are elements of the story which, though not odd or out of the way to American audiences, nonetheless have some small special relevance to Canadians.

The plot is somewhat similar to that of *Death Weekend*. Here a believably beautiful Toronto woman (Susan Keller) and her husband (Lawrence Dane) are accosted by a crude gang under the leadership of Keller's old boy-friend (Stephen Young). The husband is discommoded and Keller kidnapped. Surely in an American film of the same type the motive for the abduction would be simple lust and revenge. Here it is not so simple or so passionate. The boy-friend whisks Keller away so that she cannot sign a document putting her country home, the site of their old trysts, in the hands of developers. Foreign audiences might easily fail to perceive the blend of avarice and romance that makes this a distinctively Ontario story.

Stylistic indecision is another element of *The Clown Murders* that might be ascribed to the mode of which it is perhaps the beginning. Like so many other Canadian film-makers, Burke began in public affairs television; before that he was a newspaperman. Although he has worked in TV drama and has had one or two earlier feature projects die under him, *The Clown Murders* is his first full-length imaginative work. At least it's the first that gives the appearance of being imaginative. In truth, the story is largely inspired by the Nelles kidnapping case that, for some months late in 1969, had the Toronto *Star* and the *Telegram* vying for lurid details in the grand 1920s manner. The result is another instance of a film-maker trained to deal with fact doing a poor job with fiction.

Burke's script is a complicated and competent enough thriller, but it cannot triumph over his problems of getting actors to move about and speak convincingly. He experiences, to be kind, some difficulties with continuity and pacing. There are long stretches of slackness in which everyone seems tense but nothing happens. There's a great deal of emotional deficit spending. The cast stare intently, talk stiltedly, lose control and take off their clothes — all for very little apparent reason. There is a nice part for Al Waxman as a regional police detective given to physical and verbal understatement. His presence, however, cannot disguise the fact that behind the camera and script there must be someone of emotional depth, and that Burke, on available evidence, is not the one. He's all right on the mechanics but his actors are literally directionless. Burke has told them where to stand but has not shown them what to feel. Those are the failings that make the film trash. What distinguishes it as New Trash are the documentary bias, the current affairs urges, the Canadian cast and the inclusion of the only two concerns (quick money and lust) that mean more to Orangemen than religion and hockey.

The Canadian Forum, 1976

xiii

John McGreevy has turned out a good piece of work in his film *Beaverbrook: The Life and Times of Max Aitken*, which the CBC showed recently. The film is a docudrama. It's another of those hybrids television has developed in response to the increasing impotence of the straight documentary as a means of conveying all but the most mechanical truth. It is a form to which Lord Beaverbrook is uncommonly well suited, since the minutiae of his career are less important than his abstract failings. Still, the fact that part of the film is in documentary style has left scars on the whole. It means that McGreevy has been obliged to show the flow of his subject's life from counting-house to grave rather than concentrate on the most revealing isolated moments. It also means that he has had to take a stand either against or in favour of his principal character. He seems to have chosen the latter. But, in fairness, that has not prevented something like the real Beaverbrook from showing through.

That McGreevy is after the substance rather than the details is easily illustrated by the fact that, in what purports to be a life and times, there is no mention of Beaverbrook's dates of birth or death. Instead there is an attempt to show, first, his Canadian background (Neil Munro plays the young Beaverbrook) and, later, his private life in old age. The mature Beaverbrook is portrayed by John Colicos. It is one of the choice television parts of recent times but also one of the most hazardous. It promises the easy triumph of a one-man show but threatens, so to speak, an audience salted with next of kin. Colicos, who only months ago gave one of cinema's most embarrassing performances in *Drum*, the black exploitation movie, rises to the occasion. He does so well that it seems as though Beaverbrook's real-life acquaintances, who are interviewed between the dramatic reconstructions, are recollecting the actor at his task rather than the actual capitalist of their memory.

Surely the problem in coming to terms with Beaverbrook on film is that, despite his talent for money-making, he was a failure at everything else that interested him. He was neither hero (that's for sure) nor anti-hero, for such titles imply great symbolic importance. Beaverbrook was more important for what he owned than what he did or attempted. People aspiring to power are often more dangerous than those who have lived with it. Beaverbrook was menacing without ever reaching the top drawer of villainy. In that regard it would have been interesting for McGreevy to have placed him in the context of the other press barons.

Aitken made his first million before he was twenty-seven. He went from Maritimes bond salesman to Montreal wheeler-dealer in a remarkably short time. He was, in the second capacity, the sort of person for whom the Combines Investigation Act was written. There is little doubt that he would have had difficulty duplicating his career in a later Canada with more sophisticated financial laws.

It was his wise good fortune to cultivate the friendship of Andrew Bonar Law, who endorsed his move in 1910 to England, where he quickly won a seat in the Commons and repaid Law with a lot of dubious counsel. But then Beaverbrook was usually good at picking his friends. He spotted Churchill relatively early and, it has to be said, remained true to him even after Churchill had outlived his usefulness, save as a reputation in which to bask. The one exception was Lloyd George. Beaverbrook helped him pry Asquith from power and was repaid with a peerage. That is, Lloyd George pulled the rug out from under Beaverbrook by pretty well insuring that he would never be prime minister. Perhaps another man would have been less gullible. Certainly the other press lords would have been.

McGreevy has had to deal with the fact that Beaverbrook was prolific in many types of mischief simultaneously. He has therefore missed the point that his most characteristic role was that of publisher. Unlike Northcliffe, who practically invented the tabloid, he did not make great advances in the business. Unlike Hearst (who by American standards was respectable by birthright) he didn't crave power but settled for a good time. Unlike Thomson to come, and despite their similar background and feelings of social inferiority, he did not concentrate mainly on making money, with prestige an unearned dividend. Rather, he held onto the *Daily Express* and the *Sunday Express* as the means to vague ends he never quite realized. The papers would have been important implements to a politician, a crusader, an imperialist or an isolationist, all of which Beaverbrook was. But they could not help him decide precisely what kind of power he wanted. The *Daily Express* has been called the first classless British newspaper, the one read by (in one commentator's words) "the contemporary version of the yeomen of England." That position, however, was not a goal but a by-product of the paper's lack of direction, reflecting a similar lack on the part of its proprietor.

The (probably inevitable) failure to grasp firmly such a character is at once the strength and weakness of McGreevy's film. The docu part of this docudrama consists of interviews with survivors of an age (Rebecca West, Sir Oswald Mosley) rather than key figures in the subject's life, most of whom are now gone. Thomson, interviewed shortly before his own death last August, merely pays lip service to a fellow tycoon. John Bassett does the same; the credence he lacks as a much younger mogul is excused because he's one of the last of the breed. The best interview naturally is with Beaverbrook's biographer, A.J.P. Taylor, the only one who seems to have thought much about the subject. Unfortunately, there are no interviews with the many who rivalled Beaverbrook for the title of being his own worst enemy. It would have been pleasant, for example, to have seen Malcolm Muggeridge. Beaverbrook had him sacked from his newspaper job after Muggeridge wrote a *Maclean's* article ridiculing the Beaverbrook cult in Fredericton, which the old man strewed with memorials to his own name.

As for the dramatic parts of the film, they are exactly that — more theatrical than cinematic, set pieces relying on calm, not action, to illuminate the subject. Stuck as he was with a half-breed form, McGreevy has acquitted himself well. By failing to resolve very much he has probably come nearer the truth than he would have done by sticking to the stage or the big screen. The Beaver, as he was known behind his back, is well suited to the form the CBC has had to come up with under pressure from other media.

The Canadian Forum, 1976

xiv

The success of *Outrageous!* was assured by critics long before it opened in Toronto, its natural habitat. First there was the reaction of American observers. From John Simon to Rex Reed, nearly every reviewer of note, some of whom saw the film at Cannes, praised this modest feature about the hyperplatonic relationship between a female impersonator and a young woman just sprung from a psychiatric hospital. Audiences were similarly enthusiastic. Aware of this, Canadian reviewers paid close attention when the movie was shown as the centrepiece of the second annual Festival of Festivals (whose organizer, incidentally, is also the film's producer). They too found much to admire, and their pieces drew local audiences in large numbers.

None of this, it should be said, is very unusual in principle. In this case, though, a certain cultural point comes into play. Allowing for personal value judgements, the critics on both sides of the dotted line seemed to appreciate the film for many of the same reasons. But I would wager that the reasons why Canadian *audiences* have enjoyed it aren't the same reasons as those of ticket-buyers in the States. I can't prove this, of course, or even illustrate the point with other people's opinions. It does seem, however, that *Outrageous!* is outrageous up here and down there in two distinct ways.

Made for $167,000 and blown up from 16mm, the film is a sleeper inspired by a sleeper in another medium. The script by Richard Benner, who also directed, is based on a section of Margaret Gibson's book *The Butterfly Ward*, a collection of stories arising from her life as a schizophrenic. The book was far better received — the recipient of lavish praise and awards — than anyone would have imagined, and Gibson suddenly became much in demand as a writer. Another of the stories was filmed for television by Claude Jutra. Benner is true to the story-line of the original in that the film concerns a talented drag queen (played by Craig Russell, a drag queen, who lived with Gibson for two years) and the Gibson-like mental patient named Liza (played by Hollis McLaren) who walk a thin line in Toronto society. The former loses his job as a hairdresser when customers learn the nature of his avocation, which is impersonating Barbra Streisand, Bette Davis and the like in gay clubs. Liza conversely is, as it were, out on parole and faces reinternment in the Clarke Institute if she steps too far out of line. Their friendship is completely symbiotic. To most of the citizenry, the Russell character is a deviant and the Liza character crazy. They support each other and, together, create their own cozy milieu.

But though Benner adheres to the plot he changes the spirit of it by pursuing the bittersweet comedy and by generally making the story less of a downer than it was in print. Several critics (notably Martin Knelman and "Marshall Delaney") took exception to such alterations, stating that the script put forward the crazy-is-sane position of R.D. Laing. There is some truth to this claim, though less I believe than their reviews made it appear. In any case, it seems to me that the book was praised in Canada for qualities that would have gone unremarked on elsewhere, just as the film was eagerly gobbled up on different grounds in the United States and Canada.

Although structured as fiction, the book was a blatant statement on mental health care and written from so flatly personal a viewpoint as to be almost a print documentary. Documentaries are of course the instrument of our official culture, which has drummed into our heads the notion that they are good for us. Thus the book was warmly, officially received in much of the same spirit as CBC specials on freight rates. "Poor Gibson," people seemed to say. "She's to be pitied for being different — and applauded for calling our attention to this difference so that we can bring our records up to date."

A similar reception would have been given the movie had Benner made the film anything remotely resembling a documentary. If the film had treated Russell as an unfortunate aberration, and McLaren as a sicko — had it, in shrt, been stimulating, informative and significant — the response would have been one of official gentility — and box-office death. Instead, partly perhaps because he is himself gay, Benner treated them as perfectly legitimate people and got on with telling the story with polished dialogue and a minimum of facts. And this, I think, is what delighted (or at least surprised) an audience brought up to think of Canadian cinema as an endless series of docudramas.

Here was a Canadian film based on the truth we all know but seldom see recorded rather than on the facts in the newspapers, and one not remotely concerned with Prairie childhoods or the other circumstances by which the government, and those it has employed, try making art from tourist flakery. Here instead was a decidedly unofficial film about the urban environment in which the majority of the population actually live. And one not mainly interested in social politics, as it so easily could have been. It is clear that, as she keeps saying, Liza is naturally sane when left to her own devices and that she goes strange only when on the drugs prescribed for her stability. It would have been simple to make a statement to the effect that Ontario's system of mental health treatment is insidious: that anyone can be committed on little evidence, that class is the determining factor in who's considered normal and who's not. Such a statement is necessary, sure; but the point is that *Outrageous!* takes this for granted, just as it assumes many other truths which a documentary would have tirelessly set about explaining.

One doesn't have to be gay to know that Toronto is probably the *underground* gay capital of North America. One just has to live on the outskirts of officialdom. One need not be very observant to know also that most of what's culturally interesting in the place comes from the streets on which gays, crazies, *émigrés* and other outcasts interact and go for the most part officially unnoticed. The audience for *Outrageous!* knows this world or knows of it but seldom sees it reflected in the culture it buys. The glory of *Outrageous!*, it seems to me, is that it finally takes cognizance of the fact that whatever excitement there is in Toronto comes about in spite of the O'Keefe, the St. Lawrence Centre, the CBC, the NFB and the newspapers, not through them. The film doesn't boldly advance this viewpoint (for then it *would* be a closet documentary of sorts) any more than it peeps through the keyhole at supposed depravity and eccentricity. Rather, it takes this world at face value, using it as background against which to tell a perfectly straightforward, simple tale. Anyone who doesn't know people precisely like the characters in *Outrageous!* deserves to have his money glumly refunded.

This, however, says little of the film's appeal in other circumstances and in other venues. Many reviewers felt the highlight was the inclusion of Russell's night-club act. It comes when, towards the end, he gets a job performing in a better class of dive in New York. Personally, I am unconvinced. Martin Knelman, wisely noting Benner's commercial instinct, suggested that the film's attractiveness is the way it shows the underdog finally becoming a showbiz triumph, that it is, in effect, the story of two kids trying to get by in a world they never made and so on. This rings truer, but only from the viewpoint of camp; for *Outrageous!*, in execution as well as conception, is a 1960s low-life nostalgia film.

The exclamation point should be a tip-off. One-word titles thus punctuated — *Morgan!*, *Help!* — were to the 1960s what singers with only one name — Fabian, Dion — were to the 1950s. The style, too, indicates certain lovingly cared-for myths. People in the States seeing a film as grainy and poorly lighted as this one *expect* it to be a cult movie, little realizing this is what many Canadian films look like without meaning to. Then there is the myth of the young film-maker. Benner is an unknown who didn't come through the proper channels (the CBC and the NFB) and this is his first effort. The public, I think, is eager for proof that young talents do in fact just one day appear. They're delighted to find one, as they've so often been disappointed by hype artists who, in the end, lack in large measure the necessary goods.

All the above, though, is in a way beside the point. The fact is that Benner and the cast have made a quite likeable film. Russell, who never acted before in this sense, is natural and believable. For her part, McLaren faces the role of a mental misfit, perhaps the most difficult anyone can undertake, with the right amount of both restraint and flair. She is a sort of Canadian Sissy Spacek, not only in resembling her physically but in having that uncommon ability to elevate, by her presence, even little establishing shots and bits of linkage. Benner handles both of them amazingly well, just as he does the sets and locations. Toronto has never looked on film more like the real workaday Toronto of greasy-spoons, flats above store-fronts, streetcars, late night movies and sinister bookshops. And his script is one of those that, though involving no action, keeps from slipping into ennui. The dialogue takes full advantage of homosexual folk wit ("There's one female impersonator in Toronto," says a New York club owner, "and it's a woman"). Even when a few of the lines misfire it is, one often feels, because of some trait of the character who speaks them. *Outrageous!*, in short, is one of those films that from time to time emerges (from nowhere, officialdom thinks) and then fades away, leaving people satisfied and a bit more awake than they had been. It deserves its success but it deserves it for the right reasons.

The Canadian Forum, 1977

XV

Not that it matters much except to the backers, but God knows what American audiences will think when they watch *Two Solitudes*, Lionel

Chetwynd's film from the Hugh MacLennan novel of the same title. Chances are they will see in this drama of Quebec a technically inexpert but imaginative recreation of present realities. They might even assume the film or the novel, or both, to be controversial somehow. And from all this they could draw dangerous inferences about the Canadian film industry. The truth of the matter is that the film has an atypical advantage in lacking documentary technique, but is not necessarily better because of it. Also, though it seems by its pace and narrative balance to be a faithful adaptation of the novel, it is in fact more loyal to MacLennan's plodding than to his plot; for one thing, it stops midway through the story-line. This makes the film even less a statement on the current tensions than it would be otherwise.

To be very brief, the novel concerns Athanase Tallard, a Quebec squire at the time of the First World War who represents his village in Parliament. He's married to a lower-class Irish woman (his second wife) whom the neighbours and servants distrust as much as he himself resents the Catholic church, in particular the local priest. Foreseeing the need to bring heavy industry to his part of the province, he goes into partnership with an anglophone Montreal industrialist, Huntly McQueen, to build a mill. But he's edged out when McQueen joins forces with the church Tallard renounces. Meanwhile, his elder son is arrested when, like so many other Quebeckers, he refuses to help defend the empire. The film ends at this point, with Tallard's death. In the novel, however, Tallard embraces the church again before dying and is accepted once more by his neighbours. After that, attention shifts almost entirely to Montreal and Tallard's younger son. This son is raised as an anglophone by the Irish wife, so that he has one foot in each culture and is truly at peace in neither. Yet he decides, when the late 1930s roll around, to oppose his nationalist brother and side with those who are rushing off to defend Great Britain in another world war. That he later marries an aristocratic anglophone is intended to be a hopeful sign for the future of the country, and so on.

The novel had a considerable success in 1945 partly because the Quebec issue, incredible though it sounds today, was not much written about seriously. Other factors may have been the war fever and MacLennan's quaint conviction that the French Canadians were suffering from their Catholicism as much as the English Canadians were from their Calvinism. Although the book's cultural symbols have much less currency today, they're put to excellent use in the film, at least theoretically. Much as Joyce Wieland did in *The Far Shore*, Chetwynd uses these stereotypical characters as their own backgrounds. They're conceptual characters almost, and the atmosphere they create is more like that of Noh than a morality play; the characters are so stable than any deviation from the norm assumes great representational importance.

One difficulty, however, is that the consistency, uniformity and control of the material necessary to pull this off are not very strictly enforced in this case. Jean-Pierre Aumont as Tallard is pretty naturalistic. The same can be said for Gloria Carlin as Mme Tallard and Raymond Cloutier as the first son, Marius. But Stacy Keach, as if responding to the implausibility of his passing for McQueen the wizened old St James Street shipping magnate, gives a wildly stylized performance. Some of the supporting parts lack even this authority. Jean-Louis Roux, a cardinal, is enthusiastically demonic, as usual; Claude Jutra, who as Father Beaubien is supposed to represent the reactionary aspect of the church, could have used some of Roux's excess evil. There's quite a bit of simple miscasting here and, sorry to say, some plain bad craftsmanship.

Chetwynd has problems both as a director and as a writer. Thrice doth the boom or its shadow steal into the frame, and there is some laughable cutting. What's more, his indecision about what to do with many of the book's subcurrents leaves loose ends and banana peels everywhere. These are botched resources; another defect of *Two Solitudes* is by contrast a missed opportunity — the opportunity to capture the feeling of Montreal past, a staple setting for many of the best Canadian films along with certain periods on the Prairies.

An American with no previous Canadian experience except the writing he did on Ted Kotcheff's *The Apprenticeship of Duddy Kravitz*, Chetwynd misses the unique feel of the place and the quiet arrogance with which the English merchant princes ruled for so long. This is what the French-Canadian characters should be reacting to, the never quite openly stated feeling among the English that, though the twentieth century may belong to Canada, Canada belongs to *us*. In creating McQueen, for instance, MacLennan was trying to employ many of the traits he saw in Mackenzie King; in the film this comes down to us only in that Keach, three times and with obvious embarrassment, speaks out loud to the portrait of his mother. Chetwynd missed another wonderful shot at political statement in the bland way he uses Murray Westgate as the prime minister (Sir Robert Borden, presumably). Only Bud Knapp, in a small part as a friend of the prime minister's named Sir Rupert Irons, begins to suggest the exploitive nature of the old reality, which is what the movie should really be all about.

Cinema Canada, 1978, unpublished

NINE

The Art of Political Cartooning

i

When John Wilson Bengough died in Toronto in 1923, John Diefenbaker was an apprentice lawyer little known outside Prince Albert, and this is one of the small pities of Canadian history. It deprived us of the opportunity of seeing how Diefenbaker — with his wattles and Dylan Thomas bug-eyes, the caricaturist's dream — would have been rendered by the great pioneer political cartoonist of a nation always distinguished for its graphic wits. As it was, Bengough had to content himself with Sir John A. Macdonald, and the image he created of that lanky statesman with varicose nose and vulpine cleverness has had some influence on how history remembers him. Since the life of *Grip*, the magazine Bengough founded and in which he published most of his work, coincided roughly with the most important phase of Macdonald's political life, the two are inextricably mixed. Time and again the cartoonist satirized the prime minister in his visual editorials until at last Macdonald seemed to become one of those symbols, like Liberty, John Bull and Uncle Sam, which cartoonists use as a kind of shorthand.

But don't think Bengough was harassing beyond good taste the architect of Confederation when you view the sometimes malicious drawings that follow. It is merely that these cartoons — selected from Bengough's two-volume *Caricature History of Canadian Politics*, published in 1886 — cover in the sly fashion of the time a wide range of issues, many of which involved Macdonald. Despite the artist's prefatory notes on each, however, many of the topics he commented on in the original compilation are obscure today (these have been omitted from this one-volume selection). It is testament, however, to the pointedness of Bengough's style as well as to the continuity of history, that many of the others are still alive and as hotly debated now as a century ago. Here you will see cartoons on such familiar themes as nationalism, feminism, corruption, Senate reform and that other old stand-by, provincial rights. It was Bengough's cartoons on another hardy perennial, the Canadian Pacific Railway, that first brought him wide acclaim and made him a political force.

Bengough was only twenty-two when he founded *Grip*. He was born in Toronto in 1851 of a Scots father and Irish mother. He was one of five brothers, all of whom eventually took some hand in running Grip Printing & Publishing, an important engraving and job printing house. The family lived in the town of Whitby, near Toronto, and after finishing school there Bengough worked in a law office. Like a surprising number of other writers before and since, he decided that the legal profession did not suit his temperament and so became a printer's devil at the local newspaper, which was small enough to allow him to discover his latent talent as reporter and cartoonist. At twenty he moved to the city and went to work at George Brown's *Globe*, the most influential paper in the land, but seems to have been politically unhappy there. In 1873 he started *Grip*, which took its name from that of the raven in Dickens's *Barnaby Rudge*. It lingered until 1894, with gaps. (The bookseller Dora Hood gives the full, complicated chronology in her book *The Side Door*.) Bengough himself provided much of the editorial and graphic content, and treated with a healthy disrespect all current views except those to which he himself was committed to advancing, such as the Single Tax, antivivisectionism, decimal coinage for Britain and the empire, the prohibition of alcohol and tobacco and the case for Bacon as the author of Shakespeare's plays: the whole catalogue of nineteenth-century heterodoxy. The curious aspect of Bengough is that, for someone so political and so biting, he was surely no ideologue, not even to the extent that Henri Julien and the other cartoonists of the day were. He seems to have actually liked Macdonald, for example. A little book by Percy Ghent, *Literary and Historic Fragments of Canadian Interest: Adventures in Book and Autograph Collecting*, includes a birthday greeting and poem Bengough sent Laurier in 1908 that would suggest that Bengough never harboured an ill thought towards the recipient. As Hector Charlesworth of *Saturday Night* phrased it in a memorial article, "For many, the cheerful and kindly qualities of his temperament softened the angularity of his views."

Grip became successful almost as soon as it began appearing, thanks largely because of the Pacific Scandal, which provided natural material for Bengough at his best. His cartoons (such as "The Dainty Dish") caused a sensation. It was the turning point for Bengough as a cartoonist. When he died at seventy-two, he was considered something of a grand old man. He had published his own work in both *Grip's Cartoons* (1875) and the *Caricature History*, which includes some earlier cartoons from other sources, and had drawn for no fewer than four papers in London as well. The British editor W.L. Stead (than whom no better soul was lost on the *Titanic*) had called him "one of the ablest cartoonists in the world." The New York *Herald* had termed him "the greatest cartoonist living on this side of the continent." Thirty years after his death a bronze plaque commemorating him was unveiled in Toronto. He was the second Canadian journalist (the other was Brown's partner, Sir John Willison) to be so honoured.

To understand Bengough's work it is helpful to recall that newspaper owners had a virtual monopoly on the dissemination of news. On election nights, for example, crowds would clog the streets in front of the many newspaper offices to await the posting, in windows and on roof-tops, of returns telegraphed from distant points. Newspapers were a voice to which the people listened rather than spoke through, and which sheet they listened to was determined largely by the political party to which they belonged. Publishers were devoted to things other than truth and sometimes held office as well as the power to actually sway elections through their paper. Libel laws were invoked as often as now and with more cause — but to less effect. It was an age, antithetical to our own, in which the editorial page meant much and the sports page little. In this scheme of things, a cartoonist like Bengough, who could get away with murder by making carnage funny, was an important person indeed.

It was a time also in which technology or the lack of it, rather than the desire for a more visually fetching product, determined what newspapers looked like. Before half-tone photographs became the staple illustration, papers depended upon prolific sketch artists to record scenes or, if necessary, concoct them. Their work was printed by means of line engravings done partly by hand, and if Bengough's work seems a little overwrought by today's standards, it must be remembered that he flourished in an era when superfluousness in cross-hatching, as well as in dress and rhetoric, was normal.

Bengough's style became more intricate as he grew older. The drawings in *Grip's Cartoons*, some of which he used again in the *Caricature History*, tend to be more fluid than his later ones, but no less skilfully conceived in their premises or gag situations. In his time an ability to sketch was something cultivated and frequently used, like good penmanship, and so his panels were really more cartoons than caricatures. He did not exaggerate a subject's features as do modern cartoonists, such as Ed Franklin of *The Globe and Mail* (who sometimes resembles Bengough in other ways) or Duncan Macpherson of the Toronto *Star*. Most Canadians of the 1870s and 1880s would not have seen Sir John A. Macdonald, much less his constant photographic image, so Bengough had scant room for licence. Rather, he tried to capture the essence of the man's appearance and to match that with his political nature. It is interesting to note that Bengough's pictures of Macdonald as a middle-aged man show him, rightly, in his prime (Macdonald was fifty-eight when *Grip* began) and that it is only nearer his death that the politician in Bengough's drawings assumes the haggard appearance of the scarecrow W.C. Fields we like to connect with his shade.

Unlike most modern cartoonists, Bengough felt it was necessary to label anything that might be unfamiliar to his less informed readers or to use wordy cut-lines and titles. In our time, the editorial cartoon has grown mute except in the school headed by Sid Barron of the Toronto *Star* and Len Norris of the Vancouver *Sun*, who sequester small jokes around the page, much as Bengough often did.

What then, if the styles have changed so drastically, if today's cartoonists are much better draughtsmen, is the enduring importance of J.W. Bengough? The answers, I think, are several. The first is wit. With Bengough, a picture was figuratively worth 10,000 words, and sometimes literally as well. He was cutting and cruel but seldom inaccurate, and with only one sketch could apply more weight than a compositor with a verbose editorial in ten pounds of lead type. Also, his drawings tell us much about Canada and journalism in his time. They give us the sociological, economic and political feel of the first few decades after Confederation. They point out the ways in which we differ from our antecedents as well as the ways in which we resemble them. It is generally the differences that supply the most interest, and Bengough and the others like him are good examples.

He was not merely a cartoonist, as most of our present-day editorial artists are. He was an extraordinary man in a time of extraordinary men, of dilettantes, gifted amateurs and general practitioners who made journalism and society operate in a rather more individualistic manner than today. He was a fighter and campaigner as well as a writer of, by our standards, amazing versatility. In addition to the books of cartoons, he published several volumes of verse illustrated by himself; a political primer for children, similarly adorned; and various other works, including, the year before his death, *Bengough's Chalk Talks*, material from the illustrated lectures he began delivering a year after his magazine was founded and which brought him fame in Canada, Britain, the United States, Australia and New Zealand. He saw nothing unusual in writing songs, humour, fiction and drama as well as embroiling himself in various economic, literary, academic and political matters. (He withstood urgings to run for Parliament as a Prohibitionist, apparently feeling his independence would be compromised, but served later as a Toronto alderman.) Nor was he unusual for his time in all this. One need look no farther than *Grip*'s associate editor, Phillips Thompson (Pierre Berton's grandfather), for another example of the same breed. They were great men in a small way, and it is tempting in this book of Bengough's sketches to believe that he was dealing with his own superior breed of being, linked to us only by history and the basics of human nature. It is certainly human nature that Bengough is dealing with, and it is his understanding of it, as much as his talent, that makes him such an important cartoonist and this book such an interesting piece of the past.

Preface to an abridged *Caricature History of Canadian Politics*, 1974

ii

A remarkable change has taken place in Canadian art during the past few years, namely the sudden rise in status of the newspaper editorial cartoon from mere social criticism to respectability as a fine art. Both the Public Archives in Ottawa and the Art Gallery of Ontario have recently held retrospective exhibits of Canadian cartoons, and throughout the country such drawings have been turning up in galleries and in travelling shows. In fact, a commercial gallery devoted exclusively to such material has opened in Toronto to some success. Perhaps not far in the future is the realization that the editorial cartoon is the quintessential Canadian art-form. Not only do such cartoons sum up our obsession with politics, they also put the famous documentary bias of Canadian culture to its best use. The newspaper cartoon, not coincidentally, has been a form at which Canadians have excelled for more than a century.

An established part of this activity has been the publication of collections of cartoons by some of the leading practitioners. Those of Duncan Macpherson of the Toronto *Star* have been an annual rite for a decade now. His latest, *Macpherson Editorial Cartoons 1975*, points up all the strengths that have made him the most influential of our cartoonists. It also, though, shows better than previous compilations in memory the inconsistencies and failings young Turks in the field have taken advantage of to elbow their way into the limelight. Principal of these newer artists is Terry Mosher, a Montreal free lance, who draws under the name "Aislin." His *150 Caricatures*, the third biennial collection of his work, speaks volumes for the younger generation of newspaper satirists and also for his generation as a whole.

Macpherson's style is characterized by boldness of line, strength of composition and a visual silliness that he turns to good account in making all politicians appear to be posturing charlatans and ineffectual con men. He more than anyone else (except the Toronto *Sun*'s Andy Donato, a follower) has divorced himself from the eighteenth- and nineteenth-century tradition of meticulous cross-hatching and careful caricature. Macpherson's style reminds one of the old card game for children called Old Maid, a game that uses, in addition to the usual face cards, one with a big likeness of a bug-eyed simpleton called the Old Maid. The point of the game is to keep a poker face when this ludicrous visage suddenly pops up in your hand. The political equivalent of the Old Maid card is Macpherson's standard rendering of Pierre Trudeau. It's hard not to break up laughing at the caricature and, by extension, at Trudeau himself.

If Macpherson has kept his distance from the overblown, basically European style of caricature, he has not been so successful in avoiding the cruder, essentially left-wing kind of cartooning, what might be called the *Daily Worker* school, wherein comment is made through a stock company of stereotypes, as in a morality play. This school depicts Business (and so labels it) as a fat-cat capitalist in striped trousers with a watch-chain stretched across his waistcoat, and shows Labour (also neatly identified) as an emaciated, barefoot wretch with rags for clothes. Not that Macpherson ever descends to this level. But he does make frequent use of Everyman, a bedraggled, putty-nosed average citizen. What's more, Macpherson sometimes, when eulogizing some public figure or doing ominous panels about nuclear bombs, forsakes his cunning use of white space for some very heavy brush work. For some reason he's more prone to this antiquated style when dealing with city and provincial politics than when dealing with national and international affairs.

These are small points about small weaknesses. Macpherson's great strength is his talent for ridicule, his positive delight in making fun of whatever persons or issues stand in danger of being everywhere taken too seriously. However weak his premises sometimes are, there's no mistaking that he's more of a comedian than most editorial cartoonists; and, like most comedians, he's sometimes sentimental but usually caustic.

Even after following him for years, one finds it difficult to say with certainty what Macpherson's own political convictions are. With equal ease he will assail the conservatives and the liberals, come out forcefully against both the War Measures Act and Asian immigration. Perhaps it's merely that he works for what has been described as a small-c Liberal paper. Whatever the case, his one consistency is his treatment of politicians as bumblers, losers and worse. His Robert Stanfield, who always seems to look like a small-town undertaker, has doubtless had a real effect on the living Stanfield's career. The same can probably be said for his likeness of Trudeau, who he insists on showing in eighteenth-century court dress, clutching a nosegay. And then — and then — there is Diefenbaker, a man whose eventual gain by Heaven will surely be the cartoonists' loss. Diefenbaker, as drawn by Macpherson, looks like a goofy, toothsome Bertrand Russell reflected in a funhouse mirror. Seeing this mythical creature, one could never think of taking the actual person seriously again, let alone voting for him.

It is perhaps in some small measure the relative quietness of Diefenbaker and the decreasing sparkle of Trudeau that made 1975 less than a bumper year for Macpherson. The present collection affords only one of what might be remembered as "great" Macphersons — the kind of drawing one immediately thinks of when the subject of it recurs years later on television screens. This is Macpherson's captionless summary of Idi Amin. He is shown as a giant black frog, looking stern and somewhat mad, seated on a too-small lily pad discreetly labelled "Uganda."

Aislin, by contrast, seems to have had a good year. But then for a polemicist like Mosher, who's less topical than Macpherson and more concerned with generalities, all years are equally rich. Aislin belongs to the group of fine caricaturists (others are David Levine and the workers on the New York *Times* op-ed page) who have resuscitated the art of the nineteenth-century cartoon at its best, without that period's heavy touch and clutter. Viewed in this way, in fact, Aislin is not a cartoonist at all. He's seldom funny and is usually not meant to be. Rather, he's the spokesman for the present generation of educated radicals now so prominent in Canadian media, publishing and art. He's left wing, hip and bilingual, and he gives no breaks to people who are otherwise.

Aislin uses contempt the way Macpherson uses ridicule. Whereas Macpherson shows most politicians as fools, Aislin makes them all out as evil, menacing creatures up from the social sewer — that is, all conservative establishment politicians, who are the only ones he draws. He shows Richard Nixon, with whom he had a justifiable field day, as a dark, brooding, ill-shaven man with noticeably rodent-like ears. Others follow this pattern. There is little of Macpherson's good-natured ribbing here, only venom. Nor is there any of Macpherson's silly caricature. Aislin creates remarkable likenesses of his victims which are reminiscent of old steel engravings. Only then does he come in for the kill.

Aislin is, in technical terms, perhaps the most accomplished artist now working for Canadian newspapers. His Diefenbaker is first if not foremost a fine portrait, capturing the man's nineteenth-century roots, his legal training, his love of tradition and pomp. Only when all that is established does Aislin seem to add touches — a certain pursing of the lips, a subtle kink of the hair — which make the man look like a feeble and slightly demented turkey.

Aislin's great failure (perhaps it is also his great power) is that he lacks something for political sophistication. He is clearly not an anarchist, for he loves governments as confirmations of all he despises and would not want to see them done away with. Yet, looking at this and his earlier books, one is sure that he has only the broadest kind of conviction. How does he stand on this issue or that? How does one politico stack up against the others on the scale of imbecility? One isn't certain because the artist himself isn't certain. He lashes out at everyone to the right of himself, and does so with an unrivalled combination of maliciousness and dedication.

The last panel in *150 Caricatures* is perhaps the best summary of Aislin's idea of himself. It shows a skinny Christ tacked to the Holy Cross, his fingers aquiver as a cream pie strikes him square in the face. The caption asks: "Is nothing sacred anymore?" Editorial cartoonists — at least the best ones, and Canada has many of these — like to believe, and like to have us believe, that this is a rhetorical question.

Saturday Night, 1976

TEN
An Afternoon with Yousuf Karsh

The world's most famous portrait photographer exudes an Old World courtliness. His voice comes through the phone with an accomplished sense of graciousness. He speaks in the kind of flowery sentences one would have expected from some minor Austro-Hungarian diplomat. His pleasantly efficient secretary has announced that he is on the line, but her statement does not prepare you for the sense of talking with someone from another, more elegant era. It is the voice of Yousuf Karsh — "Karsh of Ottawa" — whose work, for more than thirty-five years, has been making the famous look great.

His telephone manner, however, does not entirely match his appearance. One half expects him to resemble his own photographs, the studies of artists, scientists and heads of state that are his stock in trade. One looks forward to velvety blacks, lush lighting and a mock beatitude. One gets instead a small, slightly nervous man with wildly expressive hands. The anecdotes, as expected, are many and polished, but in the spaces between them his conversation is halting and guarded. He has spent more than half his sixty-eight years tracking down dignitaries from Sir Winston Churchill to Fidel Castro. He is more comfortable as a recorder of celebrities than as a celebrity himself.

In fact, Karsh does not like to be known for anything other than his work, much less be judged for anything else. He greets you at the door with the old formality but once inside he is all business. He does not have with him any of the 300 pounds of photographic equipment he normally uses on his travels. Even so, he seems to arrange the interview as though arranging a portrait session. He moves a chair up close, then pushes it back, then drags it forward again. He seats himself with his back to the light so that a faintly spiritual glow surrounds his head; I cannot see his eyes. He makes it clear that he wants to talk mostly about his work, including his new book, *Karsh Portraits*. Still, when he does allow a personal comment to pass, it is sometimes revealing.

"The early years of one's life," he says, "are a tremendous influence. If the experiences were bad, one turns on them." And that may help account for both his politeness and his reticence. He was born in Armenia, in 1908, at a time when Christians such as his parents were being routinely murdered by the Turks. The bloodshed had been going on since the late 1890s and would reach a climax about the time of the First World War. In 1922, he fled, penniless, with his Roman Catholic father and Protestant mother into neighbouring Syria.

Perhaps it was the religious nature of the war, as well as his parents' interdenominational marriage, that left him with a strong interest in things spiritual. He once planned to enter the priesthood, and kidded his mother by telling her she would be the first Protestant mother of a pope. Even today he says that the historical figures he would most like to have photographed are religious leaders such as Jesus and Gandhi (though he also names warriors such as Napoleon and Bismarck). His earliest ambition was to become a physician; medical men and scientists are his favourite subjects among the living. Whatever else his early life left him, however, it left him a will to succeed, in the company of the kinds of people he's best known for photographing, "the ones who have carried on the civilization."

In 1925 — still penniless — Karsh immigrated to Canada. His uncle George Nakash, himself a photographer, sponsored him and gave him work in his Sherbrooke studio. Later, Karsh took the opportunity to work and study with John H. Garo of Boston, a famous portrait photographer of the day, in whose work one sees clearly the seeds of Karsh's own familiar style. He spent three years in the United States. It is doubtless what he learned there, coupled with the ambition he already possessed and the polish he acquired, that made him what he is: "the last of the great American heroic portrait photographers," in the words of Geoffrey James, the Canadian art critic and historian of photography.

Karsh returned to Canada in 1932 and opened his own studio in Ottawa, in a building he was eventually forced to leave when the Sparks Street Mall was being expanded. He now operates from a studio in the Château Laurier hotel. "The studio is not advertised too blatantly," he says, but then in no sense does Karsh have to advertise. He sometimes photographs for free the famous and great ones who have made his reputation. The others — less well-known citizens — pay a minimum of $1,000 for the prestige of a Karsh photograph. "For the past four or five years we have taken out a business-card type of advertisement in *The New Yorker*," he says. "It's not actually advertising, though; it is just for those who hear of Karsh but do not know how to reach him. It's very tasteful, really." He now travels about thirty-five weeks of the year. Most of the portrait work is done in the homes or offices of his subjects, so he has no studio other than the Ottawa one, with its one secretary and two assistants. He does, however, maintain an apartment in New York. There, as in London, he keeps duplicates of all his equipment.

It was not always so. Until the Second World War, Yousuf Karsh was merely a general-purpose photographer with ambitions to be rather better. "In those years," he says, without realizing what the words are conveying, "probably 95 per cent of my photographs were of women." In the years of struggle he even made one-dollar passport photos, including one for Walter

Gordon, who is still its proud possessor. It was Mackenzie King who more than anyone else helped transform the unknown Yousuf Karsh into the renowned Karsh of Ottawa.

"I chose to settle in Ottawa," he says now, "because it was a great crossroads," especially during the war. Although he concedes that Montreal and Toronto are now much greater celebrity resting places, he chooses to remain in Ottawa "simply because it is now my home." It is his home in the physical sense, the site of Little Wings, his pink-stuccoed home on the Prescott Highway, a minor local landmark, where he relaxes in the garden and exercises on the tennis court. But Ottawa also has been the home of many of his connections, of whom King was the most useful. The prime minister took a liking to the courtly young photographer and snagged many visiting dignitaries for Karsh sessions. That has led to the spurious story, repeated by detractors of both men, that King used to carry Karsh's camera bags for him.

Largely through King's intervention Karsh was able to arrange his first sitting with Winston Churchill. The time was late 1941, shortly after the United States entered the war, when Churchill was in Ottawa to address a joint session of the House and the Senate. The pictures (there were only two exposures) were taken in the Speaker's Chamber. The meeting produced the best-known of the stories Karsh is now reluctant to repeat about himself — of how, while posing him, he plucked a cigar from Churchill's mouth. It also produced perhaps Karsh's most famous portrait — of Churchill, one hand on hip, scowling like the most recalcitrant bulldog imaginable. That portrait — like much of his work in those years, first published on the cover of *Saturday Night* but reproduced thousands of times around the world — boosted his reputation out of the ordinary. The picture also says just about everything there is to say about Karsh's style and the attitudes behind it.

"These are great men, and it is up to me to build a better picture of that fact." Greatness and the inevitability of it are recurring themes with Karsh, as reflected in the titles of his books — *Faces of Destiny, Portraits of Greatness* and his autobiography, *In Search of Greatness*. Yet they are also ones full of contradictions he does not seem to have resolved. It is as though Karsh believes fame itself is a great achievement that brings with it an almost saintly glow. It is that glow he tries to capture and to emphasize on film.

"One must try to be as objective as possible," he claims. "The human face masks the true nature of the individual. I would like to think if I had photographed Hitler that the bestiality and ruthlessness would have shown through. I would not deliberately try for the inhumanity — and you can. It would have just come out." Inhumanity, of course, would also alter the reputation that Karsh maintains as the immortalizer of the lofty. "Do not go out of your way," he says at one point, "to interfere with myths." As Karsh sees it, enhancement does not constitute interference.

Karsh's portraits are carefully posed. A few at first appear to be candid

(Pablo Casals playing his cello with his back to the camera, or Robert Frost, with one leg thrown over the arm of a chair, distractedly petting a dog). Upon closer inspection, however, these too reveal Karsh's meticulous arrangement. They reveal a master, not of photography as such, but of image manipulation. His portraits do not show the subject warts and all except when the warts are part of the legend. They do not show qualities we never suspected existed, but ones the subject is famous for possessing or for believing he possesses. His thinkers are shown thinking. His poets, musicians and artists are ethereal, moody and distant. His politicians appear to have everything under control. Most of all, his famous models give the impression that they are relaxing from the mechanics of their work while continuing with it in their minds. They all give the impression of being at peace with the world, if only because they are too busy not to be. It is in this way that their myths overlap Karsh's own.

Karsh will tell you a little about his personal life, but nothing terribly revealing. His first wife, Solange Gauthier, whom he married in 1939, died of cancer in 1961. His present wife, Estrelitta, once an editor in Chicago, is a medical journalist and historian. Their house, built in 1940, is mostly glass and rests on a few landscaped acres. It has only one bedroom, so guests must be put up at a local hotel. He paints an idyllic picture of his existence, and there is no more dedicated booster of Ottawa. "I have had immense happiness there. No one more appreciates it than I."

No photographs, by Karsh or by anyone, adorn his walls, but a few favourite portraits, signed by their subjects, are displayed on a table in the den, along with photographs given him by the late American photographer Edward Steichen. For all that, though, Karsh is an inveterate and congenital photographer, not one who leaves his craft behind in the studio when he comes home at night. "I play at it just like any amateur," he says. "I play at it because I get a great deal of pleasure from doing so. On my trips I photograph the local architecture, the people in the streets. I find that it reinforces recollection afterwards. Even in my work I try to take as many candid photographs as possible. That is something some people do not seem to understand. For instance, I photographed both Karen Magnussen and Barbara Ann Scott in motion, twirling around on the ice. And then there were the photographs of cities I did for *Maclean's*."

Mainly what this tells us is that, for all his fame as a portraitist, Karsh worries as much about being type-cast as he does about accidentally revealing himself in conversation. It leads to the conclusion that Yousuf Karsh, whoever he really is in private life, is largely an unknown quantity. He would likely remain so even if he gave interviews twice daily. His alter ego, Karsh of Ottawa, whose signature is a copyright notice, is easier to pin down. He is the fellow who photographs public figures and is something of one himself. He deals in Greatness and Destiny, which are the opposite of candour, and he has been rewarded with honorary degrees, the Order of Canada and a booming sideline as a lecturer before photographic societies and museum groups around the world. Like the big names he poses and arranges, he is an institution. Like them, he does not want his myth interfered with.

His shoes shine like patent leather. His suit is a conservative grey. His initials are embroidered a half-inch high on the left cuff of his shirt, right above one of the prominent cuff-links held with tiny chains. His tie is flamboyant. He has photographed every American president from Franklin Roosevelt on, with the exception, so far, of Gerald Ford. How, if and when the time comes, will he do Jimmy Carter? What traits of personality will he seek to play up? "I think I would emphasize the spirituality and the guidance of God," he says. To say anything more would be to bring politics into the discussion, and Karsh makes clear at once that he does not discuss politics, religion or money, his own or his subjects'. "I treat every personality," he says, "as a sacred trust."

Certainly that is so in the portraits. In the anecdotes about the subjects, which eventually find their way into the texts of his books, he strives to treat them differently. Often in fact the stories seem more revealing than the photographs, though upon reflection the stories too become part of the myth manipulation process. He has photographed Richard Nixon three times, twice as vice-president and once in the White House. Was he a difficult subject, fidgety and ill at ease, the way he always seemed on television? Karsh will say nothing. One gets the impression that this time the silence is not due to Karsh's fear of lapsing into politics but rather to the fact that Nixon's myth has become a negative one. It has become an embarrassment almost to Karsh, who has stricken him forever from his registry of anecdote. He is more interested in showing that the great, like himself, transcend mere politics, religion and wealth (especially politics) even while they traffic in them.

"Castro was a very good subject," he recalls. "A very good conversationalist, too. There was no politics at all. He was interested only in the great writers of the world. We spoke of Hemingway, who was the shyest man I have ever photographed. Castro was so natural. He came into the room and removed his belt with the gun on it — the gun is a traditional part of the uniform. We chatted, though he didn't speak a word of English or French with me; there was an interpreter. You know, Tito was the same way. He spoke excellent English, but not one word of it in my presence."

His photograph of Castro is one of those published in *Karsh Portraits* for the first time in hardcover, like the ones of Muhammad Ali, Norman Mailer, Prince Charles and Jacques Cousteau. There are also new portraits of some figures Karsh has photographed previously, such as Marshall McLuhan, Henry Moore and Picasso. Mostly, though, the new book is an anthology of older photographs from earlier collections. Viewed together, the pictures reveal Karsh's amazing consistency over the years, which is perhaps a handicap as well as a triumph. The accompanying text does more than the photographs themselves to explain the reason for such consistency.

They show that Karsh is, or seems to be, in almost indiscriminate awe of everyone more famous or influential than himself.

The atmosphere in which his sessions are held is vitally important — to Karsh, the subject and the end result. "When I was in Helsinki to photograph Sibelius, he took me into his music room. 'This is where I wrote *Finlandia,*' he said. All that is very important." The photograph that issued from the meeting, however, is a frontal head-and-shoulders shot in which the composer's face expresses both great intensity and great calm: the old Karsh treatment. There is nothing to indicate that a piano was nearby, much less *the* piano. The portrait could just as easily have been made in Oslo or in Ottawa. Such familiar surroundings may have helped Sibelius relax, but one senses that their real importance was in helping excite Karsh. He likes to throw himself completely into the image he is about to enshrine. "When I made the portrait of Glenn Gould," he says, "I became so caught up that at first I forgot to press the cable release. My eyes became moist."

Karsh's stylistic consistency gives the portraits an undated quality, if not always a timelessness. In their Karsh versions, George Bernard Shaw (born in 1856) and John F. Kennedy (born in 1917) look as though they could be contemporaries. Even if one had never heard of either of them, one could be persuaded that they were engaged in some important work at about the same time in history. All that betrays the illusion are the differences in hairstyles and clothing. However much he eschews props, Karsh can do little about such differences, so he uses them to his advantage — reinforcing various myths.

Hemingway, in a famous Karsh portrait, is shown in a turtle-neck sweater. The garment appears to be one Hemingway might have been fishing in moments before. Actually, the photograph was taken at Hemingway's home in Cuba on a sweltering day. From the chest down the pullover was an expensive leather affair; Hemingway just happened to have it hanging in his wardrobe. By cropping in his mind, before snapping the picture, Karsh carved Hemingway's heroic image in stone rather than confuse us with something fresh and different.

The later visit Karsh made to Cuba, the trip to photograph Castro, would have been impossible had Karsh not been a Canadian rather than an American, as he is often presumed to be by residents of other countries, despite the way his "Karsh of Ottawa" credit line has been implanted in the world's consciousness. It was his Canadianness, however, that prevented him from photographing Mao Tse-tung, one of the greats he would have dearly loved to photograph. "It was sixteen or seventeen years ago," Karsh recalls, "that Field Marshal Montgomery sent me to officials in London to see if I could obtain documents to get into China and meet Mao. It is not commonly known, but Montgomery was one of the few westerners of the time respected by the Chinese communists. When I got to the Chinese officials, I was asked, 'How is it that Canada has not recognized the People's

Republic of China?' I never got to go." Among the living, Bob Dylan is one person Karsh still longs to photograph.

In a curious way, Karsh's work, while remaining unchanged, has become more and more topical. "During the past few years," he says, "photography has grown in status and appreciation as an art. There are many more critics, artists and collectors than ever before." In the same period, of course, Canada has become increasingly aware of its cultural resources, in photography as in all other fields. Those two facts have combined to help Karsh plan two projects. One is a book in which he will collect only his portrait of prominent Canadians. "I am trying to prepare such a book," he says. "Of course, unlike my others, it will be of interest to Canadians alone. I do this because of my great love of Canadians and Canada." The other project is more ambitious and will probably help make Karsh seem more a part of the culture with which, for all the Ottawa associations, he has never been synonymous. The project is an exhibition and a massive permanent archive of all his portraiture.

"I was in Alberta," he says. "I happened to mention that the National Museum of Australia had purchased my show 'Men Who Made This World,' which was first presented at 'Man and His World' in Montreal." The show consists of about 100 of the better-known portraits. A duplicate show, with the addition of approximately a dozen photographs of Japanese artists and public figures, has also been sold to the Japanese government. "Alberta purchased it as well. It will be on display at the Glenbow Institute and then it will travel around Alberta. Now there is also the possibility that the province will acquire all my negatives, with prints of many of them, for educational purposes and for the use of scholars throughout the world."

Another awkward pause interrupts the flow of sentences from Karsh's mouth. "Of course, I would retain control over all the material during my lifetime." Should anyone go out of his way to interfere with myths.

The Canadian, 1976

ELEVEN

Looking at the Press

i

Whenever I walk down Spadina Avenue in Toronto and pass Oxford Street, I inevitably think of Vincent Starrett, the mystery writer, editor and man of letters. Starrett was born in 1886 at 26 Oxford Street, in a flat above the Upper Canada Bible and Tract Society bookstore operated by his grandfather. Moments after his birth, it seems, he was wrapped in a copy of the Toronto *Globe* that happened to be handy (causing him to ask in later years whether any of his colleagues could boast of an earlier appearance in print). Those simple facts, I have always felt, tell a good deal about the role of the Canadian newspaper, and also about the marriage of the press and the class system, by revealing the type of family whence Starrett came and the sort of person he went on to be.

Starrett was, for instance, a genteel sort of thriller writer. Had he been a hard-boiled one, his parents would have read the *Telegram* instead of the *Globe*. Similarly, there was nothing splashy about his criticism that would suggest they bought the *News* or the *World*. Certainly there is expressed nowhere in his fifty or so books any political ideas that would have implied prenatal contamination by either the *Empire* or the *Mail*. His people, clearly, were good upper-middle-class folk, devout and concerned and liberal and quiet, just like modern readers of the *Globe*, a paper where Starrett would fit in well today (as a contributor, I mean). All of which is prelude to the obvious statement that although newspapers in Canada are well over 200 years old, the modern daily is very much a Victorian invention, a fact that is both its strength and its weakness. Such is also the conclusion drawn by reading Paul Rutherford's *A Victorian Authority: The Daily Press in Late Nineteenth-Century Canada*, a work I heartedly recommend.

Rutherford is easily the most thoughtful and best-read commentator on Canadian media history. To date, however, his audience has not been wide, mainly because his previous work, *The Making of the Canadian Media*, published in 1976, was tucked out of the way in an obscure McGraw-Hill Ryerson sociology series. Yet that was also fitting in a sense, because it is the sociology of the press that concerns him, along with its political economy. In the new book, for instance, he shines when comparing the picture of the Victorian world so familiar to us from other sources with the one reflected in local display advertising of the time. He also writes well about the effect on the press of new technology for printing and papermaking. But the real strength of *A Victorian Authority* is the discussion of the party press and its sibling, the class press, and of the way the two fit together and weave in and out. It was in the late Victorian period that the newspaper scene broke down into the popular papers on the one hand and, on the other, those that operated on a higher plane and took the world quite seriously. That division was closely tied to the adoption of party platforms supportive of either the masses or of capital.

Recently I came across a 1962 speech to the Canadian Institute for Public Affairs in which Robert Fulford bemoaned the lingering Victorian quality of Canadian dailies. Visiting a certain paper for the first time, he said, he was amazed to discover that its "equipment was all quite recent [and] the editorial and business staffs were generally young, and the atmosphere in which they worked was that of a brisk, up-to-date enterprise." That had startled him because typographically and in other ways the paper looked like it was being published about 1900 by old men. In the twenty years since then, such appearances have become more rare. (In fact, one could argue that the pendulum has swung too far and that many papers look like they're put out by kids.) Yet in the important ways, the Victorian heritage lives on in surprisingly undiluted fashion.

It's no secret that the large newspapers today are those that were the monoliths back then: the Toronto *Star* or the Winnipeg *Free Press*. Nor that most of the Victorian innovations (editorial cartoons, columnists, world news round-ups, pages of letters from common readers) remain the staples editorially. In fact, one can get quite silly listing all the carry-overs. Myself, I've always contended that most of today's printing and publishing terms speak volumes about the famous repressed sexuality of the Victorians; viz., "the Benday reverse" and "the California method," to say nothing of the shocking "over-the-transom submission." But surely the greatest heritage is the class press, which now seems even stronger because of all that has dropped away to reveal its true workings.

As Rutherford shows, there were three dimensions to the targeting of the audience, since there were self-proclaimed class papers, political papers and religious papers. No doubt there was a good deal of overlap, and some sheets, such as the Montreal *Star* in the days of Hugh Graham before he became Lord Atholstan, were all three simultaneously. The religious papers went by the wayside first; or at least, their religiosity took on an added political disguise, particularly in Quebec. But well into recent years the strictly party press was not only alive and well but even respected in some quarters. "Strong editorial comment is inseparable from party affiliation," Senator Grattan O'Leary wrote in his memoirs. "Unless it is a party press, it will not be a great press." That was less than ten years ago, when the notion was not entirely dead, if one judged by the Montreal *Gazette* or the Ottawa *Journal* or the Vancouver *Sun* (which actually had support of the Liberals written into its corporate charter).

What killed the party hackery? The common answer is that the threat of television forced the papers to grow up and to jettison their role as political cat's-paws just as they shed their shrill sensationalism. In large measure, this is quite correct. The newspapers that survived did so partly by rising above television, sometimes snootily so, and retreating into that other Victorian concept, that one about the newspaper as a fourth estate, free and uninfluenced and beholden to nothing but Truth. But there's one more element to be considered. The Liberals have been in power for all but twenty-one years in this century. There being no competition in federal politics, there is no need for any in the newspaper business. This is not to pick on the Grits necessarily. Had the Tories the same sort of record, the results would be the same: namely, the fact that you cannot be both a nation of two-newspaper towns and a one-party country and expect the party press to remain unchanged. It's for this reason, I think, that newspapers have down-played their political nature and become more and more identified with a particular class (which for some reason they call a life-style).

Toronto has probably set the pattern here, what with the up-market *Globe and Mail*, the MOR Toronto *Star* and the lowbrow *Sun* co-existing happily, each with its own distinct demographics. In the long run, the odds of survival would seem to favour the *Sun*s and the *Globe*s, with the *Star*s of this world being very tightly squeezed the past few years. Such at least is the Canadian pattern. In the United States both the *Star* equivalents *and* the *Sun* equivalents (like the New York *Post*, the New York *Daily News* and the Los Angeles *Herald-Examiner*) are suffering badly. But then, as G.K. Chesterton observed, anyone who can figure out the United States can figure out the Rosicrucians; the matter is of no concern here. The point, rather, is that while the press has changed so drastically in our lifetime it has stayed squarely within some kind of Victorian framework, so rich a legacy is that from which to draw.

In one area, however, the pattern of dependence is broken. Another new Canadian book (*The Victorian Periodical Press: Samplings and Soundings*, edited by Joanne Shattock and Michael Wolff) indirectly points up the difference. Like the Victorian magazine, the Victorian newspaper, whatever its particular pretensions and allegiances, was, to use the contemporary word, "conducted" rather than edited. It had an internal diversity, an eccentric flavour to its contents overall and in any one section in particular. Various parts of it were written for various elements within the total readership, and there was no suggestion that the business news should also appeal to the readers of the "ladies' department," or that the dispatch about the relief of Mafeking had to be on the same level, and in the same vocabulary, as the sporting news or the court reports.

Unfortunately, this idea has been almost totally lost, thrown over in favour of one-size-fits-all journalism. Perhaps the best example is the Toronto *Star*, where extensive and constant market research seems to play a crucial role in the editorial process. There are signs that other papers are increasingly following suit. If one doesn't have precisely 2.3 children and live in the right area and drive a car and make a certain amount of money, one feels like an eavesdropper. Worse, the reader often gets short-changed on those sections of the paper about which he has some special interest or knowledge. But then it's axiomatic, at least in my own heavily mortgaged habitation module, that Lord Thomson, Gordon Fisher, Donald Campbell and the others do not consult me on how they spend their millions, never have and never will, though Lord knows I'm not stand-offish. When I'm not walking down Spadina Avenue past Oxford Street, I'm sitting home close to the phone.

Quill & Quire, 1982

ii

When the federal government first announced that a Royal Commission on newspaper concentration would be held, I wrote at once to Tom Kent, the person named to head it. As a concerned private citizen and keen outside observer of the industry, I said, I should like to testify and present a brief before his inquiry. There followed a long and embarrassed official silence. Finally I received a note from the commission secretary saying that — well, er, aw — if I'd care to *post* my remarks to the commission, someone would see they were put on Kent's desk. Ottawa's response did nothing to diminish my preconceived notion that the Kent Commission was another government make-work project designed to arrive at the old and obvious conclusions. But it *did* make me follow the hearings all the more closely, with a view towards compiling a sort of reader's guide to the final report, when and if it was released. As the report was published August 18, the following chronology is intended as a companion document, a cross between Coles Notes and what I believe is called a teaching aid.

August 27, 1980. Black Wednesday. After delaying the announcement for a week so as not to draw withering fire during a premiers' meeting, Thomson Newspapers Ltd. and Southam Inc. make public the fact that they are closing down the Ottawa *Journal* and the Winnipeg *Tribune* respectively — and immediately. The timing, they contend now and later, is simply one of nature's coincidences. At the same moment, Thomson sells Southam its half interest in the Vancouver *Sun* and Vancouver *Province* combo for $57.4 million. Howls of outrage follow and various tiny screw-ups come to light. Southam's chairman, St Clair Balfour, had tried phoning the prime minister to warn him of the barrage, but the PM had already read the story in the last-ever edition of the *Journal*: the only *Journal* scoop in the memory of anyone still living.

In terms of the newspapers' traditional or recent sympathies, the

Liberals lost one in Ottawa (where they don't need any help), gained a monopoly in Winnipeg (where they surely do) and gave the Tory Southams complete control of Vancouver (where the Tories are in the same boat as the Liberals, so what does it matter?). A newspaperman phones Jim Coutts to ask what is to be done, and Coutts replies, "The only thing we can do now is give you a Royal Commission." Balfour tells *Maclean's* there may be plans for starting a third Southam paper in Vancouver so as to cushion the blow somehow. The now monopolistic Winnipeg *Free Press* prepares to jack its rate card by 36 per cent.

September. As good as its word, the federal government establishes a Royal Commission, consisting of Kent, the former editor of the Winnipeg *Free Press* and well-known Liberal; Borden Spears, former managing editor of the Toronto *Star*, the paper whose editorials Mackenzie King read to discover just what his own policy was; and Laurent Picard, the former president of the CBC, who needs no introduction and has nothing whatever to do with the newspaper business except that he reads one published in French. A few days later, on September 9, federal anti-combines people stage a raid on the offices of Southam Inc. As a result, one Southam executive, who later leaves the company, will be charged with "tearing, mutilating and attempting to hide documents." The Kent hearings commence, and Southam president Gordon Fisher and Kenneth Thomson both testify that they "discussed" the closing of the Ottawa *Journal* some months before the fact, but nothing more than that, you understand.

October. Everybody is angry with the Kent people. An executive of the Toronto *Sun* says privately, for instance, that he's been forced to reveal how much he pays for newsprint; he suspects one or more commissioners will pass this sort of intelligence on to the *Sun's* rival, the Toronto *Star*. It is said that Thomson and Southam lawyers can cross-examine witnesses hostile to the two companies but that the witnesses' own lawyers cannot cross-examine Thomson and Southam people. Everybody and his Aunt Sally testifies about the closing of the papers, the later killing of the FP News Service by Thomson, working conditions in the two companies, the relationship of the chains to Canadian Press, etc. The commission's research director refuses to talk to reporters. Speaking in Winnipeg, Gordon Fisher says newspaper monopolies may mean better newspapers since more advertising means more money to spend on editorial: a criterion by which the Ottawa *Citizen* should now resemble *The Times* of London. He also reveals that Southam once considered converting the *Tribune* to morning publication in an attempt to turn it around, but didn't bother. Peter Worthington, in his column in the Toronto *Sun*, calls all this "baloney." Later in the month, *Marketing* magazine publishes the rumour that Inland Publications, the group of Toronto suburban weeklies owned by the Bassett family, may be up for sale.

November. Matters proceed apace. Robert J. Bertrand, the director of investigations and research at Consumer and Corporate Affairs, says "merger and monopoly legislation is for all practical purposes inoperative," which everybody knows from the government's recent experience with both the K.C. Irving interests and the sugar trust. On the fifth, the Winnipeg *Sun* begins publishing, in an attempt to fill the local vacuum.

February 10, 1981. Roy Megarry and Dic Doyle, respectively the publisher and the editor of *The Globe and Mail*, are subpoenaed to testify after refusing to come voluntarily; asked whom he personally reports to within the Thomson organization, Megarry says, "I'm not really sure, and I really don't want to find out." Good man. On the seventeenth, the Toronto *Star* begins a new section called "Neighbours" for distribution in copies going to the suburbs. What's all this, then?

Ah, the twenty-seventh. The *Star*, which already owns the Metrospan chain of suburban weeklies, buys up the competing Inland papers. *The Globe and Mail* will run the story of the purchase across page one; the *Star*, however, prints its own three-paragraph press release back among the truss ads, without mentioning the *Star* connection.

March. Sensible to criticism that the *Star* interests are going to kill off some of the newly acquired weeklies to get monopolies in each important suburban community, the *Star*, on March 2, runs a long story in the first section quoting Torstar's chairman Beland Honderich as saying that the *Star* may in fact begin a regional daily, so that boroughs with one paper could conceivably be receiving two. The following day, the *Star* runs the same story again, word for word; the only difference is that in its second appearance a few extra paragraphs have been added, along with a photograph of Honderich, and that it is given even more prominent display.

A few days later, the Hamilton *Spectator*, the original corner-stone of the Southam empire, expels from its premises some researchers hired by the Kent Commission, accusing them of prying into the minds and emotions of Southam editorial employees. On the eighteenth, at the Canadian Daily Newspaper Publishers' Association convention in Ottawa, members protest the federal government's tax on "shoppers" and advertising flyers inserted in newspapers. Meanwhile, back at the hearings, Brigadier Richard S. Malone, one of the rulers of the FP chain before its sale to (and dismemberment by) Thomson, testifies it's "inevitable that concentration would lead to fewer papers in fewer hands." This is tantamount to Calvin Coolidge's remark that unemployment is the result of many people not having jobs. Still, the Brig is one of the old-timers and he never closed, sold or merged a newspaper in his life.

April. As the month begins, one notices some delightful little touches. Two former Thomson executives testify that Thomson officials routinely opened their personal mail. Beland Honderich takes the stand, and gone is the tone of last month's cloned *Star* story. "I've never learned how to operate a business that didn't produce more revenue than it spent to cover its costs," he says. "We can't continue to operate newspapers at a loss." The *Financial Post* quotes a Bay Street sage as remarking, "If I were him, I'd merge the papers tomorrow and get the flak over with at once." (In time, of course, he does just that.) In the same week, the *Star* devotes an entire page to reprinting most of a York University Gordon Lecture. The series is named after Walter Gordon, the former Liberal finance minister and current *Star* director; the lecturer is Tom Kent, who endorses the concept of an elected Senate and other pieces of Liberal party dogma.

But all this is so much prelude to the true events of the month, for now Thomson, Fisher and the other big cheeses are to have their real say, beginning on the fourteenth. Fisher explains that he tried to sell the Ottawa *Journal* nine different times, offering it for as little as one dollar, but that nobody, not Maclean Hunter, not the Toronto *Sun*, would bite. (The *Sun* confirms this the next day.) Thomson turns up and is photographed with a large hole in the sole of one of his shoes, *à la* Adlai Stevenson. Presumably the embarrassing aperture is traceable to carelessness or parsimony, but even Gary Lautens, the nice-guy Toronto *Star* columnist who usually writes about his family and their pussy-cats, is cynical.

George Currie, fired as president of FP once the company was acquired by Thomson, testifies that the Montreal *Star*, which was closed after a long strike, considered making a bargain with Southam's Montreal *Gazette* to share production facilities, on the Vancouver model, but that the plan was scrapped even though it "would have been in everybody's interest." Asked why FP continued to sink money into the Ottawa *Journal* if it was such a money-loser, Currie replies, "Obviously so we would have a card to play against Winnipeg." This is pretty damning testimony, though more surprising is Currie's remark that he was fired by Ken Thomson personally. To say the least, this is out of character. Fisher, who in fact publishes pretty good newspapers and runs his own superior in-house wire service, behaves before the commission and in public generally as though he were a man with Thomson's penny-pinching reputation, whereas Thomson carries on with such politeness, dignity and candour as to confound observers of the scene. Richard Gwyn puts the point well: "I had expected to detest him when he came to give evidence . . . But disliking Ken Thomson, let alone detesting him, is wholly impossible. He radiates niceness from every pore, down to the hole in the sole of his shoe. He's self-effacing, shy, unpretentious, soft-spoken. He peppers his conversations with engaging archaisms like 'golly' and 'gee whiz.' " Why this should be so and other abstract, almost occult questions are left unanswered when, at the end of the month, the hearings end.

Considered as public spectacle, the good stuff was over, though the mood was perpetuated in a few small straggling events. In May, the government announced that it was once again thinking of putting some teeth in the Combines Investigation Act. Yet at the same time it kicked combines watch-dog Robert Bertrand upstairs to a less controversial job atop the Anti-Dumping Tribunal. (To be sure, the government's main complaint against Bertrand was that he fingered Ottawa in the uranium cartel and also proved the major oil companies had overcharged consumers by $12 billion; but his tough stand in regard to the newspaper closings certainly didn't do him any good.)

In any event, Fisher, Currie and Thomson director John Tory were named as unindicted co-conspirators in a set of charges laid May 9 (the day after Southam announced that — surprise — there would be no third Vancouver paper after all). A special prosecutor, ironically named Thomson, has announced that they will be in court beginning September 28. To date, no suburban daily for Toronto has been announced or even rumoured, and the universe is unfolding as it shouldn't if we had any say in the matter.

Quill & Quire, 1981

iii

Those expatriate Canadian imps at the *National Lampoon* have been at it again. In a parody of *Newsweek* now on the stands, they use the excuse of a contrived press story to take swipes at Rupert Murdoch, the Australian press mogul who acquired *The Times* of London from Lord Thomson. By way of illustration, the *Lampoon* shows a front page of *The Times* as we are all familiar with it. To one side, they depict a fake Murdoch version: screaming spurious headlines on a new tabloid *Times* redone in the manner of Murdoch's *News of the World* or New York *Post*. Of course Murdoch has left *The Times* more or less alone, lest he disturb the prestige that ownership automatically confers. Yet the satire still cuts pretty close to the bone. It also, I think, raises by implication some thoughts about all the Canadian press barons who preceded this current Australian one in the consciousness of Britain and America. The subject is not often considered, even by specialists, but individual Canadians have often had a recognizable impact on the shape of newspapers internationally, though the general thrust of their influence has probably been more negative than positive.

With the possible exception of the old *Star Weekly*, which penetrated into some bizarre corners of the world, the best-known Canadian journals internationally have always been the trashier ones that seem embarrassing at home. At one time, *Hush* and *Flash*, both published in Toronto, had immense foreign circulations. I had quite forgotten how bad these were until I recently came upon some back issues in a file. "I Was Stripped Nude/Defiled in Bathtub" is the head on a Defoesque first-person narrative in the *Hush* of September 25, 1965. Not to be outdone, *Flash* of the same date blares in 144-point type, "White Guy's Lust for Black Flesh Triggers S[ex]-Bomb." More recently, other tabloids such as *Midnight Globe*, owned in Quebec, have poured in to fill the vacuum in S-bomb reportage. It may seem preposterous that such journals, to the extent they're recognized as Canadian, are the best-known Canadian ones overseas. But it's fitting in a way, since the most famous Canadian publishers abroad, though in no way really comparable to the publishers of the kind of journalism quoted above, have nonetheless always come down on the side of their own most popular instincts.

The single most important Canadian in the field is likewise the least known. George Desbarats, who's not even mentioned in any of the standard surveys of Canadian media history, was a Montreal printer who published the *Canadian Illustrated News*. He was the first Queen's Printer following Confederation. In the 1880s he and another Montrealer, William Leggo, branched into the foreign market by starting the New York *Daily Graphic*. Thanks to a process Leggo had perfected, it was the first daily to use half-tones, thus dooming the newspaper sketch artist. Such is its unusual claim to fame. But perhaps as important is the fact that it seems to have been the first tabloid daily. According to his great-grandson Peter Desbarats, the former broadcaster who is now journalism dean at the University of Western Ontario, "He apparently went to some pains to hide the Canadian ownership" of the *Graphic*, which had a short life, closing in 1889. It was not until after the First World War, when the use of half-tones for rotary presses became general and the larger cities were thoroughly dependent on mass transit, that tabloids, as we know them, developed. In this way if in no other, there is a sort of link between Desbarats's paper and the other New York *Graphic* (1924–1932), without doubt the most sensational daily of its own or any other day. Its greatest moment, for instance, came when it gave over the front page to a photograph of a murderess at the very instant of her electrocution in Sing Sing. Its editor and part owner was another Canadian, Emile Grauvreau, and I have always suspected — on no authority whatever — that Grauvreau named the paper as he did in a small act of homage to Desbarats.

Of course, Desbarats was overwhelmingly a force for the good and all the above described activity an aberration when put in the context of the two best-known Canadian press barons, Beaverbrook and Thomson, who though not much alike have come to be spoken of in the same breath, like Banting and Best or Bonnie and Clyde. Each was a distinctly Canadian figure in the way he went about the newspaper business, but Beaverbrook was easily the more complex.

For all the British associations his name now carries, Beaverbrook's is a very Canadian story. A descendant of Loyalists, he started out as a stockjobber and financier first in Halifax and then, when Halifax seemed too small, Montreal. His progress features all the hallmarks of Canadian business of his time and place, including ventures in the Caribbean. Most typical of all, perhaps, is the way that, when Montreal in turn came to seem confining, he upped and moved to Britain for to make his name. Yet while mixing in the mainstream, he also kept close to former Canadians, one of whom, Bonar Law, he was instrumental in installing in Number 10, however briefly. When he bought the *Daily Express*, he kicked all the ads off the front page and went chin to jaw with his rival Northcliffe's *Daily Mail*. His advantage, when one comes down to it, was that whereas both were following the North American pattern of catering to the lower sort of reader, it was Beaverbrook who had the North American expertise and the ability to adapt North American ideas, such as Sunday newspapers. The instruments of his will were Canadians such as E.J. Robertson, the general manager, and Beverley (later Sir Beverley) Baxter, who preceded the more famous Arthur Christensen as editor and whose son, until his death a couple of years ago, was a fixture of the *Financial Post* in Toronto. In the end, the Beaver came to seem a curiously colonial figure, eager for a life in British politics but all too willing to be bought off with a peerage; never quite certain whether he was a newspaperman or a businessman. What he was, in any event, and as Sir Litton Andrews of the Press Council once observed, was a publisher of the American sort rather than a proprietor in the British sense. He must be viewed as a person who exported some of the worst instincts of Canadian journalism and made them a permanent part of Fleet Street. Roy Thomson was altogether different.

There is now a general tendency to make fun of the first Lord Thomson because, it is widely believed, he had a distressing habit of wearing white socks and forever seemed on the verge of addressing the Duke of Edinburgh as Phil. But dumb was the last thing he was. Wrong-headed perhaps, dumb no. He saw newspapers as profit centres (an anachronistic idea except in Canada where family-controlled chains are so dominant), and he knew that the more such centres, the more profit. My favourite image of him is from David Leitch's book *God Stand Up for Bastards*. Leitch was on *The Sunday Times* when he was seconded to accompany Thomson on an official tour of the Soviet Union. He recounts a wonderful scene where Thomson makes Nikita Khrushchev an offer for *Pravda*. Ideology interested him not at all, but the old boy knew an ironclad monopoly when he saw one.

Unlike Beaverbrook, who is now a historical figure, the first Lord Thomson is still so close in time that the basic outlines of his story are familiar. He bought his first paper, the Timmins *Press*, in 1934, because he needed someplace to print radio listings, having already started a pathetic little radio station. The small papers accumulated like debris, and in time he moved into Britain seeking prestige and money. He offended with his candour, however, as when he told Dick Lunn, then a *Time* magazine stringer and now head of the journalism department at Ryerson in Toronto, that the Scottish ITV franchise was "like having a licence to print your own money." As with Murdoch after him, he bought *The Times* because doing so made him a national figure to be reckoned with. His peerage, said to have cost more than any since the days of Lloyd George, rankled others as much as it pleased him, because of the title, Lord Thomson of Fleet. In actual fact it refers to a stream in a remote part of the kingdom, though the reference is widely and incorrectly thought to be to Fleet Run, a creek which once meandered under Fleet Street but which in recent years, somewhat symbolically so, has been used as a sewer. Yet because his story is familiar it's become difficult to assess Thomson's influence on journalism.

It should be remembered, as it almost never is, that he founded *The Sunday Times Colour Supplement* and thus brought British magazine journalism into the modern world. But unlike his son, he made no mark on Canadian urban journalism, save for his brief fling with a Vancouver daily that he closed when it became a licence to lose money. In fact, he closed many papers, including some large provincial ones in England. But he also saved many smaller ones, in Canada and elsewhere, by imposing a system of sustenance and demanding mediocrity in return. He even made funny-looking dailies of what previously had been funny-looking weeklies. However, it's well to recall that, popular wisdom to the contrary, a substantial hunk of the family fortune derives not from newspapers, but from oil, or did once J. Paul Getty, so the story goes, convinced Thomson that energy was where the future lay. Yet I wouldn't be surprised if Thomson didn't have some basic understanding of the unique importance of newspapers after all. He was, in any event, a big-timer. One cannot help but make the comparison to figures like Pierre Péladeau, who owns *Journal de Montréal* and *Journal de Québec* and who failed to export himself in 1977 when he opened a paper in the States, the Philadelphia *Journal*, which closed in short order.

They were curious people, these press lords by whom, unfortunately, the rest of the planet knows Canadian journalism. They were willing to accept instant recognition by purchasing salient institutions like *The Times*. But what they really contributed was a zest for over-sized photos and tabloid scandal-mongering at the expense of anything better. Curiously, these traits weren't then much in evidence or very successful back home. It was as though they felt restrained in Scottish Toronto or Scottish Montreal and went to Britain, not only to be wealthy where it counted, but to be naughty where it didn't matter — in much the way people used to sneak away for weekends in Buffalo.

Quill & Quire, 1983

TWELVE

A Supplement to the *Supplement To The Oxford Companion to Canadian Literature*

Linsey-Woolsey, Leonard W. (1921–   ), grandson of Robert W. Linsey-Woolsey, minister without portfolio in the Borden government. Born in Wilberforce, Ontario, which his Loyalist ancestors helped to settle, Linsey-Woolsey was educated privately until his nineteenth year, whereupon he attended a succession of universities — McGill and the Sorbonne, among others — at all of which he was taught beyond his ability though not necessarily beyond his intelligence. The reception accorded abridged publication of his London School of Economics dissertation entitled *Patterns in Imperial Trade, 1850–1948* was such as to persuade him to remain in Britain, lecturing and philandering. Upon his return to Canada a few years later, he became, like the last worthwhile member of many another old Ontario family, a historian. In that sphere, his works, which are distinguished by the timeless grace of his style and the caution evident in his conclusions, include *The Orange Order and the Making of Metropolitan Government* (1963) and, most especially, *Profiteers and Expostulations: The Banks, the Pulpit, and the Press on the Home Front During the First World War* (two vols., 1967, 1970). The second volume, based partly on papers held within the family, received the Governor General's Award. More recent is *Auto-Festschrift: Essays in Honour of Myself* (1982). *A Man in My Position*, memoirs of his private and public lives, is scheduled for publication imminently, though to date has been seen in widely scattered excerpts appearing in journals. Linsey-Woolsey has sat on numerous government panels and inquiries.

Loftus, Susan (1942–   ). Born in Croydon, Ontario, Susan Amelia Loftus first came to prominence while a student at the University of Toronto, where she won the coveted Peregrine Acklin Prize for Verse and did important work in the field of trivia. Although she edited the student magazine, *The Lanthorn*, it was only somewhat later that she first became interested in the possibilities of mixed media creations and the potential interchangeability of talent from one discipline to another. Thus it was that, while a postgraduate, she brought out her first collection of poetry, *Black Marshmallows*, and produced her first film, *Envy*, which was recognized at once as a breakthrough effort in the film-maker's struggle to employ grainy half-images and dissonant lighting in the retelling of urban folk myths. Since that time, Loftus has been active as a musician and puppeteer as well as a writer, and is regarded as one of the most serious exponents of fusing popular culture and political statement. Her later books, most of which combine collage and prose poems, include *No Man's Land* and *Short Term Grants*. She is currently artist-in-residence at the Brockville Public Library.

Nicholls, Drake (1941–   ). A key figure in culture for more than fifteen years, Nicholls was born in Torytown, Quebec, and emerged on the scene in the middle 1960s as one of the editors of Muskeg Press, where he was instrumental in the publication of now classic works such as *The Human Worm* by Paul van Neff and *Rimes of a Second-Class Citizen* by Madelaine Charbonneau. With the sale of Ryerson Press to foreign interests in 1970, his energy was rechannelled into cultural politics, first as media liaison with the Bookmen to the Ramparts Committee, then as executive assistant to the interim president of Emergency Action for Children's Librarians Now and later still as managing director of the Small Publishers of Peace Coalition. All were groups with the avowed purpose of, in Nicholls's own celebrated phrase, "bringing the government down to our level." Subsequently, he was named cultural policy consultant to the city of Ottawa and then to the province of Manitoba, before leaving to become research co-ordinator of the Royal Commission on Private Funding in the Arts (the so-called Whelan Commission). When the commission tabled its report in 1981, Nicholls found a permanent niche in the public service as staff resource person to the principal undersecretary in the federal Department of Cultural Affairs (Theatre). So far as is known, he has never written a word.

Postlewaite, Warren T. (1934–   ). Born in Wormwood, Saskatchewan, and educated at the universities of Minnesota and Manitoba, Postlewaite has himself acknowledged that he is "a major critic, though perhaps a secondary writer of poetry and fiction." It is well to remember, however, that his sprawling *Honeysuckle* (1970, reissued 1972) was termed "a work of the Duddy class" by *Jane's Book of Canadian Novels*. Similarly, his *Departmental Ditties* (1969), verses about academic life presented in the Service tradition, has never wanted for readers and remains a popular assemblage on curricula and with the educated public generally. A wide-ranging teacher and scholar, Postlewaite has held positions at several larger institutions, including the University of Lethbridge, where he founded the school of didactic studies. He has usually brought outside attention to bear on such places as he has been affiliated with, through his frequent contributions to the quarterlies and the better popular magazines. More recently, he has been associate professor of talent at Glacier Community College.

Smith, Kelso (1946?–?). Born in Mission, British Columbia, Smith is the most daring of the experimental poets associated with the famous literary magazine *Rumpus*. His early work, appearing mostly in that journal and in others such as *Tongue-tied* and *disequilibrium*, is gathered together in a number of pamphlets and chap-books issuing from his own publishing house, Pants Press. These titles include *Dialogue With My Body* (1969) and *If Only Dogs Could Play the Clarinet* (1970). Subsequently he edited the short-lived bilingual journal *Hautejinx*, before undergoing a literary transformation that seems to have been connected to a religion he founded based on the colour green. Thus, at the beginning of this second and equally productive phase of his career, we find him bringing out such works as *Crucifacts* (1976), a volume of concrete poems on inspirational themes, and *Holy Smoke!* (1978), which displays continued preoccupation with the same concerns but is expressed in more traditional diction. In 1981, Smith withdrew from the literary world and indeed seems to have vanished from society as a whole. In recent years, he has acquired a large cult following, whose members believe, variously, that he has met a mysterious death, been imprisoned in Mexico or entered a monastery to lose weight. *Wasted*, an autobiography of which he is putative author, was published in Vancouver in 1983 in an edition of twenty-five *hors commerce* copies printed on rag paper made exclusively from old tuxedos. Specialists, however, consider the text to be spurious.

Westerbridge, Roderick R. (1916–   ). Born in Entreville, New Brunswick, Westerbridge established himself as a critic and seminal influence shortly after the Second World War, in which he served with alacrity and some distinction. It was as one of the "war writers" that he first arrested the attention of his contemporaries. This group, which so shocked the post-war society with its biting satire and willingness to deal more or less openly with the question of sexual candour, published several works. Of particular and lasting interest is the joint collection of verse, *4 Poets 4/4 Poetes 4*, in which Westerbridge, Val Mason, Pierre Johnson and Luke McMahon preface selections from their works with sections in which all the co-authors interview one another about the creative process. Subsequently, Westerbridge has produced many other books and has edited several key anthologies, as well as publishing at his own expense the influential review *Standards* (1958–1970). The title was drawn from a line in one of Westerbridge's best-known poems, "Dance Against the Guttersnipes," which concludes: "and I run/ out into the snowbanks/ screaming Standards! Standards!/ but no one hears."

Quill & Quire, 1982

INDEX

King, W.L.M., 15, 25, 117, 139
Klein, A.M., 56
Knapp, Bud, 117
Knelman, Martin, 113, 115
Knister, Raymond, 65
Kotcheff, Ted, 117

Lampman, Archibald, 64
Lapointe, Jean, 90
Laurence, Margaret, 83
Laurier, Sir Wilfrid, 15, 120
Lautens, Gary, 141
Law, Andrew Bonar, 111, 144
Lawrence, D.H., 15, 44
Layton, Irving, 47, 48, 55, 62-64, 67, 75
LeBourdais, Isabel, 92
Lee, Dennis, 48, 55, 62, 72-76
Leggo, William, 143
Leiterman, Richard, 93
Leslie, Kenneth, 79
Levertov, Denise, 23
Lévesque, René, 88
Liberty, 35
Lightstone, Marilyn, 105
Livesay, Dorothy, 52-55, 65
Lloyd George, David, 111, 144
Loiselle, Helene, 90
Lombardo, Lou, 99
Lomez, Céline, 106
London *Daily Express*, 111, 144
London *Daily Mail*, 144
London *Sunday Express*, 111
Lord, Jean-Claude, 91
Lunas, Jeffrey, 105
Lunn, Dick, 144

Macdonald, Sir John A., 26, 29, 119-121
MacDonald, Wilson, 16, 65
MacEwen, Gwendolyn, 51
Maclean's, 67, 112, 130, 139
MacLennan, Hugh, 116-117
Macpherson, Duncan, 121-125
Macpherson, Jay, 55
Magee, Michael, 100, 101